The Economics of the Nigerian Civil War
and Its Prospects
for National Development

The Economics of The Nigerian Civil War And Its Prospects For National Development

By

NWABEZE REUBEN OGBUDINKPA
Senior Lecturer, Department of Economics,
University of Nigeria

Fourth Dimension Publishing Co., Ltd.

First Published 1985 by
FOURTH DIMENSION PUBLISHING CO., LTD
16 Fifth Avenue, City Layout. PMB. 01164, Enugu, Nigeria.
Tel+234-42-459969. Fax+234-42-456904.
email: fdpbooks@aol.com, fdpbooks@yahoo.com
Web site: http://www.fdpbooks.com.

Reprinted 2002

© 1985 Nwabeze Reuben Ogbudinkpa

ISBN 978-156-280-3

CONDITIONS OF SALE

All rights reserved. No part of this publication may be reproduced, stored in a retrieval system, or transmitted in any form or by any means, electronic, mechanical, photocopying, recording, or otherwise without the prior permission of the publisher.

Photoset and printed in Nigeria by
Fourth Dimension Publishers, Enugu.

PREFACE

The post Civil War Nigeria has attracted an array of books on the historic and political aspects of Biafra's secession. As if by design, such works have invariably painted nothing but a pessimistic picture of the civil war. However, lurking beneath the pessimistic picture is a burning question. And this question is, "Did Nigeria derive any economic benefits from the civil war?" It is in search of the answer to the above question that this work was undertaken.

It may appear strange in a developing society like ours where many see war as destructive to find the author of this work talking of gains from destruction. However, being a dispassionate analyst, he intends to explore this neglected aspect of the Nigerian Civil War. The latter will complement the pessimistic aspect of the war already existing (Madiebo, 1980; Nwankwo, 1972; Cervenka, 1971), and thereby provide an efficient forum for evaluation of the civil war.

The author is highly indebted to many, too numerous to mention, who directly or indirectly have made this study possible. The few selected for mentioning because of the uniqueness of their contributions include The University of Nigeria Senate Research Grant that financed a part of the study, Dr. Acha Ndubisi, Professors S. Kodjo and C. Nnolim who read the draft and made illuminating suggestions with assiduity, Professors M. Ikeme, E. N. Ugochukwu, Dr. H. O. Uwaegbute and Mr. "Uzummuo" who helped to focus attention on the essentials of this research, and Mrs. C. R. Goodson who typed the draft in a possible publishable manner.

Finally, I must show my gratitude to my wife and children who gave me not only time away from my home responsibilities but helped me to foot my bills so that I may travel out of Nigeria to use library facilities. However, whatever defects or weaknesses that this work may have are solely my responsibilities.

Nwabeze Reuben Ogbudinkpa

NOTE:

No part of this work or research may be reproduced in any form or by any means without the prior written permission of the author.

Nwabeze R. Ogbudinkpa

To my late son and daughter

                        Chukwuma

                                    Ogbudinkpa

                 Chinenye

TABLE OF CONTENTS

CHAPTER   PAGE

I. WAR CONTRIBUTION TO TECHNOLOGICAL ADVANCE: A UNIVERSAL SHOCK PERSPECTIVE   1
    Merits and Demerits of War, 3

II. NIGERIAN FEDERAL ARMY'S CIVIL WAR STRATEGIES, CONSEQUENCES, AND IMPACT ON THE BIAFRANS   7
    Strategies to Subdue Biafra, 9.
    Consequences, 10. Impact of the Strategies
    on the Biafrans, 10.

III. BIAFRAN ARMY'S CIVIL WAR STRATEGY AND INDUCED TECHNOLOGICAL INNOVATIONS AND IMAGINATIONS: A CLASSIFICATORY ANALYSIS   16
    A. BIAFRA'S WAR INDUCED MECHANICAL INNOVATIONS   17
        Hand Grenade, 18. Bombs, 20. Guns, 20.
        Bullets and Cartridges, 21. Mortars, 22.
        Helmets, 24. Rockets, 26. Mines, 28
        The Biafra Beer, 28. The Footcutter, 30.
        The Coffin, 30. Ojukwu's Bucket, 32.
        The Flying Ogbunigwe, 34. The Biafran
        Shore Battery, 34. Armoured Vehicles, 36.
        The Gunboats, 37. Battery Reactivator, 38.
        The Biafran Bush Refinery, 39.
    B. BIAFRA'S WAR INDUCED CHEMICAL INNOVATIONS   *41*
        Military Oriented Chemical Innovations, 41.
        Explosives, 42. British Gun Cotton, 42.
        Propellant Powder, 43. Quasi-Military
        Oriented Chemical Innovations, 44. The
        Biafran Bush Refinery, 44. Super Petrol,

CHAPTER	PAGE

Kerosine and Diesel, 45. Engine Oil, 47.
Brake Fluid. 47. Civilian Welfare Oriented
Innovations, 47. Distillation of Alcoholic
Drinks, 48. The Making of Soap, 52.
Salt Production, 54.

C. BIAFRAN WAR INDUCED INNOVATIONS —
FOOD, FEED, MEDICINE, CLOTHING, AND
SHELTER   56
Food, 57. Food Production Directorate, 58.
The Land Army, 58. Research
Centres, 59. Animal Protein, 59.
Food Processing and Packaging, 60.
Animal Feed, 62. Medicine, 66.
Clothing, 67. Shelter, 68.

IV. LINKAGES OF BIAFRAN TECHNOLOGICAL INNOVA-
TIONS IN POST CIVIL WAR NIGERIA: A SEARCH   71
   i. The Federal Military Government Period, 1970-1979, 71.
   ii. The Federal Civilian Government Period, 1979-1983, 75.
   iii. Specific: Linkages of Biafran
        Technologies in the Fourth National
        Development Plan Outline, 78.
        Engineering technology, 78.
        Chemical technology, 80. Welfare
        Promoting technology 81. Shelter
        technology, 83. Enactment:
        Austerity cum Anti-Smuggling, 84.

V. BASES OF FEDERAL GOVERNMENT ATTITUDE TO
INDIGENOUS TECHNOLOGY: A SPECULATIVE TRIP   88
Economic Constraint, 89. Psychological
Constraint, 89. Technological Con-
straint, 89. Sociological Constraint, 90.
Administrative or Institutional
Constraint, 91.

SUMMARY   94
BIBLIOGRAPHY   95
INDEX   97

CHAPTER I

WAR CONTRIBUTION TO TECHNOLOGICAL ADVANCE: A UNIVERSAL SHOCK PERSPECTIVE

War, which is a definitely horribly organized ancient armed means of settling dispute, is a deleterious inherent social legacy to the modern world with grave consequences mostly on the disputants. War often is the last resort when all attempts at peaceful negotiations fail. In the words of Von Clausewitz (1976)[1], war is an act of violence intended to compel our opponent to fulfil our will. Implicit in the last statement is a Latin expression "si vis pacem bellum para" which says that if you want peace you must prepare for war. War is a prunning hook instituted by nature to curb mankind of evil. The war of any community always starts from political motives; for the latter is the objective sought and war is the instrument or means to achieve the objective.

A point implicit in the above assertions is the statement that war is an utterly unnecessary evil which befalls a society because of the irrationality and overambitions of both their political and military leaders. Many people have voiced pronouncements against the use of war as a tool for settling dispute. Those who have experienced it have not minced words in expressing hatred of it, but it is very unlikely to disappear from the face of the earth as ritual murder and slave trade have done. This is because it is very difficult to eliminate and or control once it breaks out; for once it breaks out, other forces at work in a society collaborate to make complex its control and elimination.

There exists today in the world many statements which condemn war. Some have merely denounced it as an inhuman and absolute means of settling political disputes. But such a denunciation is as irrelevant as denouncing malaria with out trying to wipe out malaria causing mosquitoes or as denouncing poverty without trying to raise the real national product of an economy per capita. Among such condemnations, there exists a very scathing one which is, that it interferes with the progress of those establishments designed to cater for quiet and peaceful society. This scathing charge is brought out by Von Clausewitz who envisioned war as the most dreaded of the four horsemen of the apocalypse, namely war, famine, pestilence, and death, riding stirrup to stirrup to cause human misery and political change (Michael Howard and Peter Paret ed.,[2] 1976). From the above perspective, many critics or hardliners if you like, of war as an instrument of dispute settlement contend that war might be regarded as a nemesis for national blunders and abominations.

There is no question that the above view of war is very pessimistic, artificial, and therefore unbalanced. Such a view no doubt would find support in the nineteenth century dogmatic belief which theorizes that war can never be anything but damaging. And one being carried away by the idea of catastrophic destructions of lives and property congruent with fighting a war should no doubt see anything but good in belligerency. The Japanese war makers in the latter part of the last century apparently were an exception. They foresaw the good effects of war and deliberately fostered wars so as to bring about the beneficial consequences. Likely beneficial consequences that the war condition may elicit are especially technological and, to some extent institutional. Anthony Leeds pointed out that the innovational aspects were strikingly clear in World War II and are drastically changing human life today (Jules H. Masserman, ed. 1963)[3]. Such innovations may contribute to directional equilibria or new equilibrium states through the feedback of the innovations into the system. In this sense, the innovational functions of war contribute to change, re-organization, and evolution, and may because of the special conditions of the war increase the rate of development and adaptation to new circumstances.

Having seen the above mentioned benefits of belligerency, and realizing that most analysts of war often ignored them it behoves this study to speculate that such analysts were acting in a mentally unbalanced state of reasoning. They should therefore not be blamed for the pessimistic pictures of wars they painted; for they were suffering from onetrunk mindedness.

Unquestionably, a totally optimistic and unmixed view of war as opposed to the pessimistic one painted up above is out of the question as far as this analysis is concerned. The latter, the hardliners' pessimistic view has failed because it has stretched its point too far by not seeing anything good about war. Their view has failed to recognize the catalytic role which war plays in economic progress. Though those four horsemen of Von Clausewitz apocalypse are sporadic and separate in appearance in developing economies, there is no doubt that war-induced advance in technology for annihilation purposes has been the precursor for civilian technological progress in advanced countries. History stands to show that the state of military shock sharpens thinking, and the latter is a prerequisite to technological progress. Present-day examples are the United States of America and Israel who have subordinated thinking and eco-social ambitions to one major goal, military superiority over their adversaries. They have adapted and modified their old technologies to meet the challenging war needs of the present times. The inevitable is multidirectional technological advance beneficial to both the military and the civilian. War, therefore, stimulated and aroused them from their slumber so as to innovate and meet the pressure of their adversaries. This last statement is in agreement with Howard (1976)[4] citing of H.G. Wells uncharacteristic panegyric of military virtue which, among other things, include determined regular, and farsighted research in science and technology. To give specific examples, many civilian conveniences of fifty years ago have not changed one bit today. A house of today is still as ill-ventilated as that of fifty years ago; nor have our standards of living changed much significantly. In contrast, a riffle used in a battleship of fifty years ago is nothing to write home about; for it is inferior in power, speed, and convenience to those of today. No one has any need for such a superannuated tools. Its best home is the museum. If we then abstract ourselves entirely from either the pessimistic or optimistic view of war, and cut the middle road, we shall be governed by Adolf Hitler's idea which accepts war though as an evil is a pruning-knife for the pruning of a sick bough. And for a society to be always healthy, there should be occasional pruning; that is, war which shocks and induces an economy into technological innovation and progress.

A warning about this work that is called for at this juncture is that this work should not be misconstrued as an advocacy for war. Far be this as the intent of this work, for only a psychically maladjusted individual would entertain this type of intention. And the author of this work is not one. The author is perfectly in agreement with Saint Augustine who sees man as devoid of natural intentions for war but fights only when anarchy causes an aberration from his peaceful norm. In other words, what this work wants to make clear is that everything that happens has its advantages and disadvantages, and war though heinous is no exception. We should not allow our biases to blind us in such a way that we shall be incapable of presenting an objective and balanced picture of war. War has merits.

Merits and Demerits of War

Accepting the fact that war has merits and demerits, this work argues that the demerits, being generally the visible destruction of lives and property clearly observable in the area of a country that has experienced war, are most often recognized. The merits such as bringing into use so-called marginal resources, the development of agriculture based on seed-uses in the "marginal" foot-hill hunting-and-gathering areas of the fighting communities, the exploitation of old resources and new resources in new ways, the special case of war innovations, the redistribution of labour both quantitatively among old uses and qualitatively among new labour uses are not often recognized and mentioned. This is because these merits are not generally very obvious. One ought to know that the qualitative redistribution of labour among new labour uses is extremely significant where rigidified labour distributions impede the development of labour saving innovation present in the society prior to the state of war. Based on the above analysis this work accepts the implicit belief that the most progressive technologically minded countries of the world, to mention just the United States of America, the Union of Soviet Socialist Republics, Japan, Korea, Taiwan, and Israel, had been economies which at one time or another, and or even now, torn by wars.

The main thrust of this section is not on the obvious demerits of war. Rather it intends to concentrate on the often unrecognized positive merits of war — the commendable resultants from war shocks. They are found in every war no matter how primitive. One has to probe very deeply and hard into any war with a balanced mind so as to find them.

Diverse perspectives of the merits of war exist today. They range from the theologian-moralist view which sees war as a check on man's pursuit of sinful, selfish motives rather than public interest, to the Hegelian psycho-philosophical contention that war is a means of checking the pugnacious, frustrating, temper-tantrums and biting sarcasms of nations. It is a necessary evil for the restoration of a nation's ethical health by preventing corruption and thereby ensuring eternal peace. It is an antidote to evils and chaos between nations. It is the final court of appeal in world history (Leon Branson and George Goethal eds. 1964)[5]. A politico-historian, like Alstair Buchan, (1966)[6] conceptualizes the merits of war as deriving from the fact that nations and governments being what they are, have been known to be relaxed most often but occasionally obstinate and egocentrically naive of their own apparent rectitude. War provides a therapy for this malady. Besides the aforementioned merits of war is the obvious eco-technology. There is no gainsaying that war quickens the demolition, reconstruction, and rehabilitation of an otherwise dilapedated parts of the country if such parts are war affected. This is because once a nation has experienced a war, it tends to eliminate the scars of war so as to obliterate the memories of the war. It is from this point of view that Summer has branded war the main agent of effective change within a nation. War also stimulates eco-technology ideas which, when a return is made to a calm, moral, and political environmental set-up, conduce to scientific research and technological advance, all geared towards increased production. The inference deduceable from this last statement is that war is an agent to military technological advance, and the latter has reverberations on civilian technological progress. Certain large scale civilian economic activities of today are incontrovertibly intimately fused up with military policy. War needs have led to research and success from which civilians have gained in the form of improved civilian gadgets, building materials, and pharmaceutical products. One area where such civilian technological gain is very obvious is in civilian or commercial aircraft which has its basis in early military aircraft. The implication from the above revelation is that there exists the possibility of tapping war knowledge for the perfectability of the economy provided an economy maintains a pragmatic reconciliation of civilian and military objectives. From this perspective, this study infers that the eco-techno view of the merits of war is a propitious road to rapid and increased production, to internal or national power and progress. It is the knowledge of this that has led to accustomed devotion of a reasonable percentage of national resources to military preparedness or defence in countries like the United States of America, the U.S.S.R., France, and Israel to mention but few. Because these countries are growing faster and faster, one who concludes that there is a high positive correlation between military preparedness and economic growth may not be wrong. In actual fact, the U.S. assigns between 8% to 10% of its GNP to the military sector.

This work has in generality alluded to the possible meritorious technological contributions of war. The author wonders, therefore, why many preceding writers on war have shut their eyes on such gains by concentrating only on the demerits of war. This writer considers their works futile or even wrong analysis because they are unbalanced. Such writers would have made their works balanced by including among their enumerated demerits of war the fact that war attendant distress and brutalities induce research necessary to render the enemy powerless or impotent. This indulgence in research is the result of a shock created by war. The inevitable from such research is technological innovation. And to the extent that the latter succeeds, the overall technological plan of the warring nation will rise. For this reason, this part of the study concludes that war is not commendable, and should never be commended; but whenever it inevitably occurs, it should be recognized as modern technological innovation-inducing force. War induced technological innovations improve the civilian technological plan of a nation. In conclusion, war should never be allowed to occur; however when it inevitably occurs, the societies that have experienced it must try to get the most meritorious results out of it.

References

1. Von K. Clausewitz, *On War* (Washington: Infantry Journal Press, 1950).
2. Michael Howard and Peter Paret ed., *Carl Von Clausewitz: On War*. (New Jersey: Princeton University Press, 1976).
3. Raymond Williams, *The First and Last Things* (N.Y. The New Thinkers Library, 1964), pp. 155-157.
4. Anthony Leeds, "The Functions of War" Violence and War", Science and Psychoanalysis Vol. VII, New York, Grune & Stratton, 1963, pp. 60-80.
5. Leon Branson and George Goethal eds., *War: Studies from Psychology, Sociology, and Anthropology* (New York: Basic Books, 1964). pp. 198-199.
6. Alstair Buchan, *War in Modern Society: An Introduction* (London: C.A. Watts and Company Limited, 1966) pp. 82-97.

CHAPTER II

NIGERIAN FEDERAL ARMY'S CIVIL-WAR STRATEGIES: CONSEQUENCES AND IMPACT ON THE BIAFRANS

A historical fact is the eruption of a civil war in mid 1967 between the rest of Nigeria and the secessionist sector of the same country which, in mid-1967 by unilateral decision, chose to be known as the independent economy of Biafra*. One should not blame the leaders of the so-called Biafra for unilateral independence, for Ian Smith of Rhodesia left them a cue when he unilaterally declared Rhodesia independent of Britain on November 11, 1965. The war which followed Biafra's secession was a gruesome one that lasted almost three long years. It was a war that attracted little or no positive sympathy for Biafra both from either many African countries or the rest of the world simply because of the unique setting of the stage for the war. This civil war provides a basis for speculations as to what a similar war might have for other developing economies of the world if they take similar action.

It has to be remembered that already treated Chapter I envisaged war as a universal shock that propels warring economies into quest for technological advance without mentioning any specific economies. This chapter narrows the focus to war shocks during the Nigerian civil war. It confines its interest to Federal Nigerian Army's Civil-War Strategies, and their consequences or impact on the Biafrans.

A credible remark at the initial part of the work is that Nigeria had certain pre-civil war nationalists, like late Herbert Macaulay, Dr. Nnamdi Azikiwe, late Ahmadu Bello, and Chief Obafemi Awolowo, who have worked relentlessly and meticulously to bring together heterogeneous groups of people to become a country.

Their efforts came to a climax with peaceful granting of political independence in 1960 by Britain. The only sad thing is that their hard-earned independence did not last up to a decade before it ran into difficulties that

---

*Biafra as used in this work was a defacto economy lasting only between mid-1967 and closing 1969. It took its name from the Bight of Biafra found at the eastern coastal part of pre-1967 West African maps. As far as this paper is concerned, Biafra no longer exists except as a historical concept.

culminated in the civil war. A prerequisite to a comprehensible treatment of the issue required in this chapter is the need to examine man-made and nature-given flaws that inhere unnoticed by the pre-civil war nationalists. Many analyses of the civil war precede this one, such as the works of (Madiebo, 1980[1]; Cervenko, 1971[2]; Nwankwo, 1972[3]; Oyinbo, 1972[4]; and Ojukwu, 1969)[5], to mention but few. Their common fault is that they have either ignored entirely such flaws or, where treated at all, have simply glossed over them as inconsequential.

A prerequisite to analyzing the Federal Nigerian Army's Civil War Strategies is a thorough analysis of the man-made and nature-given flaws inherent in pre-independence Nigeria. The first root cause of the civil war hinges on the amorphous character of the major ethnic groups that constituted pre-civil war independent Nigeria. It ranged from the easily implemented brutal murder temperament of party opponents common with the Yorubas, to the arrogant, grabby tendency and touting cowardice habits of the Ibos, to the suspicious tendency of the Hausas of the actions of other major ethnic groups, no matter how good intentioned they might be. These flaws no doubt would exist in a predominantly feudal agrarian economy lacking equanimity and complacency with which people treat each other. And pre-civil war Nigeria was one such economy (Howard, 1976)[6]. Secondly, there are basis to suggest that Nigeria was brought together to be a country not by appreciation of the indispensability of one another but by outside force which by use of adroit strategies made its presence and role in the country indispensable. To perpetuate its presence in the post-independence Nigeria, the above ulterior motivated force at the least opportunities harped on the explosive weaknesses or dissimilarities of the newly independent country such as the existence of ethnic suspicions and dominations, real or fancied religious antagonisms and intentions of the constituent elements of the country, and the existence of skewed progressiveness in education, civil service and domination within the country. These emphasized rather than closed, widened rifts in the newly independent Nigeria. Thirdly, the search for the root cause of the civil war must transcend the above seemingly obvious factors to the more subtle factors that began to gather momentum years before the actual eruption of war. Definitely, petty political bunglings in the Western Nigeria in particular and the rest of the country in general disproportionately and adversely affected the Northerners, Westerners and Mid-Westerners. The result was the hatching and nurturing of hostile feelings and intentions, phobia and psychic disturbances in ignorant people. The inevitable vaguely-understood hostile expectations were easily manipulated by war leaders and incompetent politicians willy-nilly under the guise of nationalism. They conditioned the masses for war by pointing at dissimilarities among the sectors of the country. The coup d'etat of 1965 being badly implemented served to strengthen the charge of domination proffered by the outside force. A scapegoat was sought to deal with the supposedly villain and this was provided by Biafran secession in mid-1967. No doubt, a war would never have been fought if emotionalism and irrationality during crisis had not fired the masses with hatred. While the Biafrans underrated the injury which their arrogance and grabby tendence has caused on the rest of the country, the Federal Nigerian war lord was ignorant or guilty of having only a sheer knowledge of indigenous technological capability of Biafra.

Strategies to Subdue Biafra

War is characterized by absence of love and only a fool would think otherwise. One should, therefore, find several conventional and unconventional strategies being deployed to subdue Biafra. Bearing in mind that the Nigerian war leader called the civil war a twenty-four hour surgical police action, conventional strategy was adopted initially during the war. This consists of sending armed troops into Biafra with definite instruction not to shoot but to parade and chant war songs to frighten the Biafrans into renouncing secession. This tactics rather than yielding the expected dividend, served to harden the determination of the Biafrans never to go back. There is no place where the biblical statement, that he who has his hand unto the plough need not look back, is more true than in the then Biafra (H. G. Mays & M. Metzger, 1971)[7]. None of the two sides to the civil war has accepted firing the first shot. But definitely shots were exchanged. This led to the Federal Army's adoption of a more destructive conventional equipment like tanks, grenades, mortars, machine guns, bombs, and rockets. The invasion and destruction of lives and property that followed was a real holocaust. But Biafra remained unshaken.

The second strategy which the Nigerian Federal Army mounted to suppress Biafra was a war of propaganda. The media were used to dish out information, both true and false, to confuse the Biafrans and to elicit the sympathy of the outside world while real war was going on. This tactics yielded the Nigerian Army the greatest dividend. It prevented many nations from sympathizing and recognizing Biafra.

The third strategy was creating hardship by encirclement and blockading Biafra. The pressure that this strategy brought with it was immense. It resulted in loss of farm land and crops, shortage of locally produced and imported goods essential to human life. This can be called the use of hunger as a tool of war. Its unconventional classification lies in that it made not only the Biafran soldiers to suffer but also Biafran civilians had more than their due shares. Their welfare really suffered.

The fourth strategy which the Federal Nigerian Army used against Biafra was the twisting and tangling of war and non-war needs purposefully to create a lot of socio-economic, politico-humanitarian problems. This strategy restricted the operation of international relief organizations like the Red Cross, Caritas, and the World Council of Churches in Biafra.

One more strategy which beat the imagination of the Biafrans was the unprecedented though historic and unholy alliance of two ever-opposing forces, the Capitalist Britain and the Communist Russia, in a conspiracy to help the Federal Nigerian Army to destroy the underdog, Biafra. Possibly the Federal Nigerian Army solicited their collaborations. Possibly they offered to help voluntarily. But the essential thing is that such an unholy alliance was used. It could be construed as a conspiratory alliance being used in what might be called a euphemistic brawl. And the magnitude of the civil war would not have been what it was but for the use of this alliance as a strategy. Biafra was offered by the Federal Army as a play ground to the alliance, and their indiscriminate bombing and touts created panic, hysteria and frustration not to mention the inevitable holocaust.

Consequences

In a short work such as this, it may not be possible to treat all the consequences of the strategies adopted by the Federal Nigerian Army on Biafra. However, an attempt must be made, and the ones to be dealt with are the most serious.

It can be said that the strategies served to harden the Biafrans. They lent credence to Biafra's belief that more than unity was the issue under dispute. Apart from human sufferings, and economic deprivations, they helped arouse the consciousness of a people to the immense crude technological endowment or talent indigenous to the area.

One more additional consequence of the strategies is to compel the Biafrans, crude and refined scientists alike, to begin to experiment. This statement follows from the notion that whoever is rejected, never rejects himself. Therefore, the strategies led to improvement in Biafra's indigenuous technology. And the following section will deal with this issue.

Impact of the Strategies on the Biafrans

The Biafran civil war confronted the Biafrans with a host of military problems. But at the same time, it brought with it a host of problems of sociological, economic, humanitarian, geographic and political nature in an environment where nature is generally lenient and man relaxed. These problems compelled the people of the area to relinquish their relaxed and indolent attitudes, rack their brains for the solutions to their immediate pressing needs. The drive to solve these problems invariably yielded the Biafrans a certain degree of success. It is only from this perspective of success that the impact of the Federal Nigerian Army Civil War Strategies on Biafra to be analyzed in this section is to be appreciated and recommended for Nigeria's good.

Generally, the impact of the strategies of the Federal Army's Action was on increased war demands. Such increased Biafran government-war demands were concentrated mainly on tools to fight the war. They included items such as metal industrial products, those of allied manufacturers of munitions, those on ship building, those certain textile products employed for army uniforms, on raw food and processed food products, as well as curative and preventive medical products. These mainly war demands twisted and tangled with non-military economic needs of the civilians.

One wonders why the author takes a diametrically opposed stand to the pessimistic impact of war generally employed by earlier analysts of the Biafran secessionist war, and envisions the impact as yielding positive contributions to Biafra which, when assimilated by Nigeria, may help the country. However, it has to be made clear without equivocation that the author consider them as positive miniscule contributions comparable to Anatiano's two grains of wheat hid in a bushel of chaff which one has to search hard to find. (Griggs, no date)[8]. The irksomeness of searching and finding them might have been the reason why earlier analysts of the Biafran civil war had treated this aspect of research with levity.

That certain impact of Federal Strategies on Biafra are positive contributions to Nigeria's health is unquestionable. The first positive impact came as a result of besieging the defacto economy. Besieging, a synonym of blockade, prevented foreign manufacturers from getting into Biafra. The inevitable or resultant consequence of the blockade was the shortage of not only war materials but also of civilian consumer goods. Biafra witnessed rises in prices of inputs and products of unprecedented nature, with the former rising faster than the latter. the sequel was the shrinkage of the profit margin. This state of affairs stimulated Biafran entrepreneurs and research institutes into experimenting with local raw materials and indigenous technologies in a manner and with a tempo as had never been witnessed in the history of the besieged area. There occurred thought stimulations to solutions of war created problems. The lesson learned from the above is that difficulties stimulate thoughts, and the latter are pre-requisites to technological innovations.

It should be pointed out that no war exists in Nigeria now nor is the author advocating a real war and blockade so as to foster technological advance. Instead what the author is advocating is a de-facto war and blockade. The nation should act as if war really exists and impose import restrictions, implement austerity measures in those areas where there are local alternatives, however crude they might be. Having tasted the refined products from the technologically advanced countries, and being cut short of supplies, and being confronted with crude local alternatives, blockade would inevitably stimulate efforts to improve the qualities of the local alternatives. Acute vision shows that this will be a welcomed road to Nigeria for rapid technological progress.

Another positive impact of the strategies on Biafra was the stimulation of confidence in self. Many technicians, craftsmen of pre-war Biafra lost confidence in their ability to compete with imported goods. Being forced by war to take to inward looking rather than outward looking, for the means of sustenance and fighting the war, the Biafran scientists, crude indigenous scientists, local craftsmen, and technicians exhumed the area's indigenous technologies. Their motto was, "do your best for your young country." Typical indigenous technological innovations that occurred in the then Biafra were found in utilizing local resources to produce war materials, civilian and military apparels, curative and preventive drugs, and fresh and processed food to mention but a few. Such innovations formed one of the answers to the Federal Army's use of import restriction and economic blockade as a weapon of war.

From this point of view, it can be said that the civil war had done Biafra in particular and Nigeria in general some economic good. It aroused and released latent and dormant energy in the Biafrans for technological advance. Its economic importance are focally dual. First, it showed that the Biafrans and other developing nations can advance technologically if left alone. Secondly and ironically, it showed the existence of local technologies which can be harnessed to serve as pedestal for still higher technological progress which one day may be comparable to those of the advanced countries. And where Nigeria adopts them and perfects them, the economy will benefit immensely in the form of reduced losses of hard earned foreign exchange.

The third impact of the strategies on the Biafrans is the adoption of the strategy of replication. There were instances where proven indigenous basis of technology did not exist. What the Biafrans did was either to import such technologies either by military captures or through smuggling from certain saboteurs or federal soldiers sympathetic to Biafran course, dismantled, studied, and replicated them. One may argue that this road to technological advance is illegal. However, if the illegality comes up as a question, the author feels that all technologically advanced countries of the world are equally guilty of committing illegal acts. For the Russian submarine has been caught racing to the scene of an accident of an American sophisticated war plane in the Atlantic under the pretext that it was going on a rescue operation but with the ulterior motive to copy the American technology of building such a plane. On the other hand certain Americans have been jailed in the Soviet Union for spying on certain of Russian productions and technologies. Even of recent, Russia has shot down a South Korean commercial plane (Washington Post, September 5, 1983)[9], on the ground that it flew over sensitive technology area and is being used as a decoy for American spy mission. Suffice it to say that apart from the above examples of attempts at illegal acquisition of foreign technologies, other examples applicable to other countries abound. The Federal Nigerian Civil War Strategies have made Biafra reveal to Nigeria one avenue, a not highly delectable one of course, of improving its technological base. That is getting it by crafty devices.

A warning implicit in the Biafran example for Nigeria is that the latter should not embark on indiscriminate replication of foreign technologies. It is only those that answer to the needs of the economy that should be acquired for replication. The Biafran scientists used a lot of such technologies to prove, if given a chance, what technological capabilities they have for Nigeria.

The fourth effect of the strategies on the Biafrans was the instilling of discipline and perseverance very central to technological progress. Just as actual wars and the ghosts of wars have induced the already advanced countries to progress technologically, so they have directed scientists of secessionist Biafra to use local resources and initiatives to conduct research and produce means of checking the invading Federal Army. There is no restriction on using the war era research findings for peacetime civilian technological progress of Nigeria. Though we may not replicate the above type of discipline and perseverance in peacetime Nigeria, yet this effect of the strategies is a pointer in the right direction. And Nigeria has to conduct a research on socially acceptable means of instilling discipline and perseverence in its subjects.

We have read very much (Madiebo, 1980[10], Nwankwo, 1971)[11] how the civil war has retarded Nigeria's technological progress. For example, a popular saying is that the civil war has set Nigeria 50 years back. However, if we realize that the GNP of the warring nations rise faster during hostilities than during peace time, then we must come to the conclusion that there is something economically good in war. From this point of view it can be speculated that one of the impact of Federal Nigerian Army's Strategies on Biafra was to unleash a dynamic force for action. The above in conjunction with Sombart's (1913)[12] discovery and revelation of the revolutionizing power of war is a prima facie case against economic negativism in the analysis of war such as has been adopted by earlier analysts of the Nigerian civil war. It is a proof that the civil war has technological economic advantages which post civil war Nigeria should tap. The war has provided pressure which served as a motive force or powerful impetus to technological innovations. That war pressure is a strong motive force is also confirmed by John (1954-1955)[13], who saw government demands for war supplies as favourably affecting heavy metal and capital goods industries without contraction in other forms of economic activity. Even Ehrman (1953)[14] shared John's view when he showed that there is a high correlation between the needs for war and technological advance. The Biafran achievements though under socially unacceptable conditions seem to support their assertions.

To an inquisitive mind, many questions appear implict in the above analysis. Certain of such questions are the following: Has the civil war had any contributions to make towards Nigeria's technological advance? Did the civil war prove anything relative to Nigeria's technological capability in future? Based on the events in Biafra, could one safely say that the nuclei of technological progress exist in Nigeria though they are not widely recognized? In the face of the Biafran proven technologically capability of Nigeria in certain areas, is the present Nigerian government to be commended for still importing certain such foreign technologies? What lesson has the country learnt from Biafra's blockade and consequent technological achievements? Is there a way in which the above lesson has influenced the country's future plans and aspirations for technological advance? It is in search of the answers to the above questions that the forthcoming two chapters are set.

References

1. Alexander A. Madiebo, *The Nigerian Revolution and the Biafran War* (Enugu, Nigeria: Fourth Dimension Publishing Company Limited, 1980).
2. Zdenek Cervenka, *The Nigerian War 1969-1970* (Frankfurt am Main: Bernard and Graefe Verlay Fur Wehrwesen, 1971).
3. Arthur A. Nwankwo, *Nigeria: The Challenge of Biafra* (Enugu, Nigeria: Fourth Dimension Publishing Company Limited, 1972).
4. John Oyinbo, *Nigeria: Crisis and Beyond* (London: Charles Knight and Company Limited, 1971).
5. Odumegwu C. Ojukwu, *Biafra: Selected Speeches with Journal of Events* (New York: Harper and Row Publishers, 1969).
6. Michael Howard and Peter Paret ed. *Carl Von Clausewitz On War* Princeton, New Jersey, Princeton University Press, 1976), p. 1.
7. Herbert G. Mays and Bruce M. Metzger, *The Oxford Annotated Bible* (RSV) Luke IX Verse 62 (New York: Oxford University Press, 1971), p. 1259.
8. William Griggs, *Shakespeare's Merchant of Venice, The First, (The Worst) Quarto* (London: William Griggs, Hanover Street, Peckham S.E., 1600), pp. 5-6.
9. *Washington Post* September 5, 1983.
10. Madiebo 1980 pp.
11. Nwankwo 1972 pp.
12. Werner Sombart, *Studien zur Entwicklungsgeschichte des Modernen Kapitalismus II Krieg und Kapitalismus* (Munich, 1913), p. 13.
13. A. H. John, "War and the English Economy 1700-1763" *Economic History Review,* Second Series VII 1954-1955; pp. 330-34.
14. John Ehrman, *The Navy in the War of William III 1689-1697* (Cambridge: Cambridge University Press, 1953), p. 174.

CHAPTER III

BIAFRAN-ARMY'S CIVIL WAR STRATEGY-INDUCED TECHNOLOGICAL INNOVATIONS AND IMAGINATIONS: A CLASSIFICATORY ANALYSIS

Wars and the rummors of wars are a shock to many in the technologically developing economies. This is because many vicious changes like financial chicanery, logistic maneuvering, brigandage and piracy are always attendant on waging wars. If we were to take the above pessimistic though artificially unbalanced view of war wholesale, we shall unfortunately lose sight of the catalytic and admirable technological innovations which violence and wars usually generate. The above picture of war found in developing countries is doubtlessly alarmist, though based on the intractability of the aforementioned war-induced vices and on the paucity of well documented war analyses. This study is a deviation from the above alarmist picture by envisaging war as a spectrum of group conflict that promotes both military and non-military technological innovations.

In veering away from the pessimistic view of war, this study sees the latter as one if not the strongest often neglected stimulus to technological advance. This statement hinges on many empirical observations of instances where wars and technological innovations have twisted to influence each other as well as general economic progress in a nation. The case study chosen to show how war and technological innovations twist to influence each other, and promote economic progress is the Nigerian Civil War, alias the Biafran Secessionist War.

Chapter II maintains with a certain degree of confidence that the Nigerian civil war yielded to Biafra certain technologically economic advantages. However, previous analysis of the civil war shied away from analyzing them. Speculating on the causes of their failures lead to the conclusion that their reticence might be attributed to the intractability of this area of war analysis. To venture into this area, one is confronted with the onus of proving beyond reasonable doubts that technological innovations had really taken place in Biafra during the civil war. Furthermore, an additional damper to the attempt might be attributed to possible repressions, in the form of lack of recognition, from the already technologically advanced nations; the more so as appropriate supportive proofs are either non-existent or where existing, are held as classified official secrets. But be it as it may, an attempt to do so must be made and it is on it that this chapter is all about. Hopefully, many observations as well as logical, and tangential comments exist as pointers to the bases of proofs. (Madiebo, 1980)[1].

A warning is appropriate at this point. It is that if the yardsticks of the advanced countries are used to evaluate Biafra's crude war technologies, the latter would not pass as creditable achievements. But evaluated in terms of other developing economies, then secessionist Biafra, now an entity within Nigeria has achieved creditable technological advance. Furthermore it seems likely that innovative ability in certain developing economies may have crude innate bases which can be visioned in handicrafts like carving, weaving, moulding, casting, welding, and fabricating of various kinds. It can be nurtured and improved from infancy by education and training. Such has been the case in secessionist Biafra.

A. BIAFRA'S WAR-INDUCED MECHANICAL INNOVATIONS

One fact of the Nigerian Civil War was the occurrence of seemingly many innovations in the field of mechanical engineering in the blockaded and wartorn Biafra. If these are accepted as significant technological innovations, they seem to bear testimony to the often heard expression that necessity is the mother of inventions. And in Lane's (1958)[2] expression, giving such innovations top priority is a sure route to rapid economic progress. It may not be possible in a short work as this to give an exhaustive listing and analysis of the ramifications of this aspect of Biafran technological achievements. An inquisitive mind who is ready to explore more than this study can present is, therefore, referred to books on the Nigerian civil war, like that by Madiebo (1980)[3], Cervenka (1971)[4], and several issues of the war era Biafran Sun (1965-1969)[5]. This study intends to take only the major cases of such technological innovations for detailed analysis. Furthermore, though many authors were responsible for different innovations, the writer wants to attribute each to one innovator, a ghost innovator known as "Uzummuo"; that is "Fairy Smith."

That real innovations were made in the war-torn Biafra is attested to from the news release by Dr. Nnamdi Azikiwe, the first President of the Federal Republic of Nigeria who, then as an amazed Biafran exclaimed that technologies developed during the civil war were sequel to the hardships borne by the Biafran population (Markpress Release, Biafra, February 29, 1968)[6]. Dr. Azikiwe's release is reminiscent of a saying popularly attributed to Adolf Hitler which is claimed to be saying that war brings out the best in people.

"Uzummuo" the Biafran ghost innovator was an indigenous illiterate innovator who harkened to the desperate but clarion calls of the secessionist Biafran government to its subjects to use the high level manpower and resourcefulness rediscovered during the civil war to help the blockaded economy to withstand the strain of hostilities. Let us assume that many modern engineers in the then secessionist economy initially had no faith in "Uzummuo's" ingenuity. However, since the de-facto Biafra had no world recognition and therefore no help from outside its area of claim, it was in a situation where assistance even from hell was accepted. The modern engineers had no choice but allow the illiterate ghost innovator to try. They joined him as such innovations manifested signs of success. Nevertheless, he was the kingpin in every technological innovative endeavour. Having gathered men of his thinking and imagination, most of whom were illiterates with innovative power and determination in a selected government-provided underground workshop, "Uzummuo" led his men in tinkering with every mechanical device that would help check the powerful Federal Army. Their perseverance led to the following mechanical innovations:

i. *The Hand Grenade*

Diligent toiling night and day in an environment disciplined by the fear of an invading army soon began to yield fruitful returns. The first success which "Uzummuo" scored was in designing and producing an "udala" i.e. oval shaped Biafran hand grenade. The specimen was fashioned out of a hollow cast-iron filled with locally-made explosives and small metal balls. The prototype Biafran hand grenade was so designed that it fragmented or exploded at the expiration of a reaction time of two to five seconds. Figure 1 shows the specimen of a typical crude Biafra's hand grenade. In a way, the above grenade could be regarded as a miniature anti-tank and anti-personnel bomb only useful for short-range attack.

In assembling the constituents of the hand grenade, "Uzummuo" carefully fitted a delay-action fuse at the broad end, otherwise known as the head, of the "udala" shaped explosivefilled cast iron before linking the fuse to the tightly corked explosives in the cast iron by thread. Launching the hand grenade for action requires removal of the delay-action fuse with the teeth before throwing at an on-coming enemy. As the fuse is removed the cast iron is scratched by the wire on the fuse, and the scratch sparks the explosive soaked thread. It is likely that "Uzummuo's" innovation provided the secessionist Biafran soldiers with increased firing power and protection as well as the means to clear suspected enemy bunkers and trenches. Its effective use against either enemy's tank or personnel put either out of action.

Though a success, the hand grenade had the unique disadvantage of being

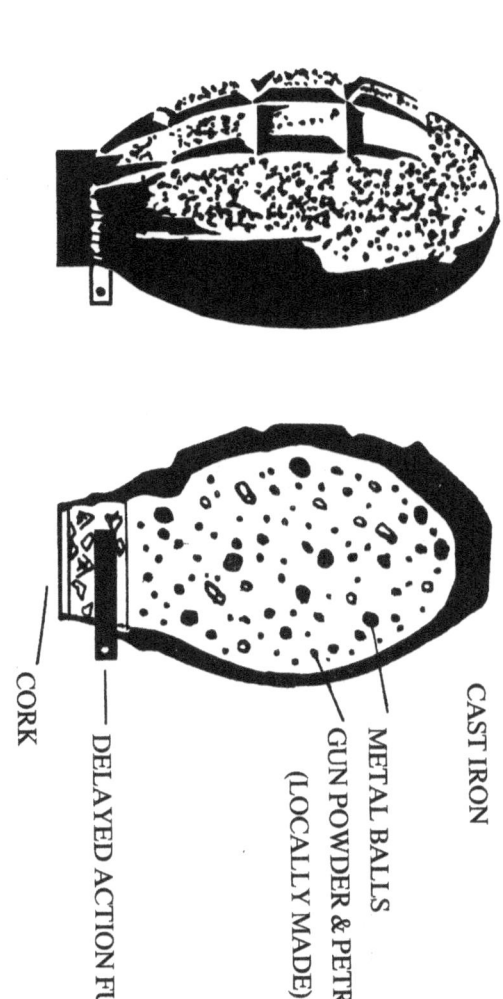

Fig 1.

SPECIMEN OF BIAFRA'S HAND GRENADE

CAST IRON
METAL BALLS
GUN POWDER & PETROL
(LOCALLY MADE)
DELAYED ACTION FUSE
CORK

effectively deployed only at close range. It was also very crude. Imbalancing of the product made it more often than not, to miss its target. However, to the have-nots like the Biafran soldiers, irrespective of the disadvantages, the innovation added more courage to their fighting valour. But it has to be remarked that one of the things which the advanced countries carefully and discreetly kept out of reach of the developing countries is the technology of manufacturing destructive equipment like the hand grenade. No doubt, the reason is that they might use them irrationally with least provocations by their neighbours. Given such a precaution, one wonders how "Uzummuo" and his crew came by the formula? One can speculate that it was as a result of sheer military blunder of the Federal Nigerian Army. It was pointed out in Chapter II that one impact of the Federal Nigerian Army Strategies on the secessionist Biafra was the stimulation of replicative spirit. The Biafrans having captured one such foreign supplied grenades gingerly defused it. After studying the components, "Uzummuo" and his crew used improvised local raw materials to produce the Biafran "udala" shaped hand grenade.

The economic significance of this technology to present Nigeria is that the country can produce with local resources detonators to be used in mines and road constructions. Apart from the above mentioned gains, the local production of such grenades by the Nigerian Army, since they are used for military training, will save the country a lot of foreign exchange which would otherwise be spent on imported foreign ones. It is only from these two points of view that the economics of this technology derive.

ii. *Bombs*

One can consider the Biafran innovation of the hand grenade as a pointer in another direction — the making of bombs. The techniques of making both are similar except that the bomb is generally larger and designed to explode either by percussion or time mechanism. It has to be pointed out that the innovation of the bomb based on local raw materials did not much help the secessionist Biafra especially as it lacked a thrower or aircrafts. Its increased production and effective use had to wait for the acquisition and modification of the "Minicon" aircrafts, alias the Biafran Babies to carry and drop them on targets at low altitudes. (Madiebo, 1980)[7]. Without bothering with repetitions, all that can be said is that the technology of bomb making will have the same economic significance to Nigeria as making the hand grenade.

iii. *Guns*

Besides hand grenades and bombs, another type of technology which the Strategies of the Federal Nigerian Army drove the defacto Biafra into was in the making of guns. It has to be pointed out that technology of gun making was not new in the area known as secessionist Biafra. The blacksmiths of Awka and many blacksmiths in the Railways Corporations at Enugu were known to have produced dane-guns used for hunting in pre-civil war era. However, for the Biafran soldiers teetering under the fear of the encroaching armed Nigerian troops, it was obvious that the locally made dane-guns were more than inadequate. In their dire need for a better war instrument than the dane-guns, "Uzummuo" and his crew found some bases in both smuggled-in Chinese rifles and captured Soviet kalashnikov automatic rifle from the Nigerian troops (Cervenka, 1971)[8]. Having dismantled and studied some of such rifles, they innovated the crude Biafran automatic rifle nicknamed "the Helicopter" because of its resemblance to the helicopter as it dangled on the shoulder of a tired Biafran soldier. "Uzummuo" also innovated a magazine, a reservoir of cartridges, by first casting the mould on sand. The magazine when attached to the "helicopter" made the latter a recoiling magazine equipped twenty-round automatic rifle. Though an innovation to be reckoned with, the "helicopter" had the unfortunate disadvantage of being exceptionally of low range; it never performed effectively beyond a few yards.

"Uzummuo" and his group also ventured to innovate the double-barrelled gun by replicating it from the pre-civil war acquired double-barrelled guns in Biafra. Whether this can really be called an innovation in view of the previous knowledge of dane-gun production is an issue that this study does not want to examine. Nevertheless what they did was to dismantle, study and reassemble some of the available double-barrelled guns. Using the knowledge thus gained and a little ingenuity, they diced the barrels out of old car steering rods, welded such two rods together, carved the gun butts out of the common iroko hard wood. The assembled components yielded the locally made Biafran double-barrelled gun. Except for the crudity, and finish, the above gun did not differ much from the imported counterpart.

"Uzummuo's" double-barrelled guns did not feature much as a fighting tool during the civil war for two reasons. First, they suffered from low range like the dane-guns and the helicopter. Furthermore, as the Federal Nigerian Army tightened its blockade on the secessionist, the latter increasingly ran short of its stockpile of imported cartridges. Many of such guns had to be set aside to wait for the innovation of gun cartridges later.

Guns and especially double-barrelled guns had been a symbol of affluence in many parts of pre-civil war Nigeria. This being the case, guns had been a source of foreign exchange leakages. The economic importance of innovation in this area is that local industrial production, though must be Federal Government seriously supervised and controlled, would help to close the gap to foreign exchange leakages. It is to this extent that the economic importance of this war-era innovation derives.

iv. *Bullets and Cartridges*

One aspect of Federal Nigerian Army's Strategies on the Biafrans was the production of bullets for sophisticated guns from the advanced countries. While Britain and the Soviet Union supplied the Federal Army with sophisticated guns like Mark IV, certain unscrupulous European gun-running merchants also were busy supplying the secessionist Biafra with certain of such guns with deceptively limited quantities of ammunitions (Ojukwu, 1969). The war would not have lasted so long were it not for these sources of arm supply. Early morning raids on unsuspecting Nigerian troops by the Biafran soldiers (an unconventional war tactics of course) armed with home-made weapons scared the Nigerian troops and gave the Biafran soldiers an opportunity to collect their loot and get away before the more numerous and more powerful Nigerian soldiers would round them up. Such loots included such guns mentioned above.

After using the bullets that came with the looted guns, a problem soon faced the secessionist soldiers, for blockade and federal might prevented their replenishment from abroad. Lack of recognition added an additional dimension to the seriousness of this problem. Being in such a fix and determined not to give up fighting, the secessionist Biafran government turned to and found a solution in "Uzummuo" and his men. The latter having studied the circumferences of the above sophisticated guns, adjusted their drill machines to produce bullet butts which could suit the sophisticated guns. By filling the butts partially with explosives and attaching either spherical or conical lead missiles to the butts, the group innovated the bullets with which the Biafran troops continued the war.

The economic implication of this technological innovation to present Nigerian Army is that if the innovation is utilized, it will reduce significantly the shortage of bullets which the army needs in the training camps. Just like the other aforementioned innovations, it will reduce foreign exchange losses due to foreign dependence for supply. It is also possible that the production will boost employment both military and civilian in the economy not to talk of improving the country's technological base.

It has to be pointed out that cartridges were similarly produced as bullets. But this study prefers leaving the analysis of the technology till the treatment of Chemical technological innovations. This is because of the higher chemical requirements in cartridge production. The following Figure 2 shows a specimen of Biafran cartridge only.

v. *Mortars*

One fact of the civil war in the Biafrans was that the Federal Army's incessant shelling produced numerous psychoneurotic conditions in soldiers ex-

Fig 2.

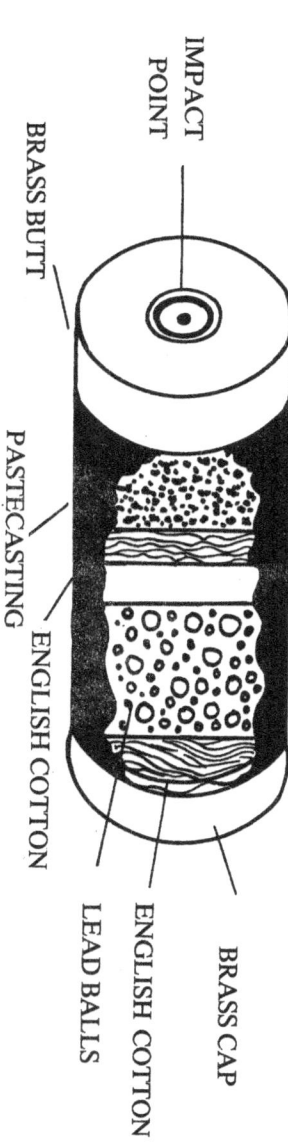

BIAFRA'S GUN CARTRIDGE

posed to shelling. To retaliate from the above Federal Army's form of attack, "Uzummuo" the quasi-scientist and his crew and the write-ups on mortar production interpreted to them. After studying the 6 x 81 mm and 6 x 3 inch mortar barrels inherited from the pre-civil war Nigerian First Battalion stationed at Enugu, the group by trial and error used local resources to innovate small mortars. Their innovations were mostly short-range, low-muzzle velocity but high arch trajectory contrivances for throwing pyrotechnic bombs. Madiebo (1980)[10], referred to the use of such mortars at Nkpor junction battle. On the other hand the Markpress release (Biafra, April 16, 1968)[11], also attributed the destruction of a convoy of 102 Nigerian vehicles at Abagana to the action of a locally made mortar.

It is very hard to prove the above claims. It might be possible that the above attacks were made by smuggled mortars into Biafra by foreign mercenaries; and there were many of them on the Biafran side. If it was possible that the secessionist Biafra produced mortars, the economic significance of the latter to present Nigeria would be like those of aforementioned mechanical devices.

vi. *Helmets*

Apart from the offensive and defensive innovations in weapons referred to above, the Federal War Strategies compelled the Biafran scientists to experiment with the production of protective helmets which would shield the soldiers from the shrapnels of the Federal Army's guns. The head is often the best target during hostilities and, therefore, must be protected. Any shot that gets the head is more likely to lead to death than one that gets on any other part of human body. It therefore became the first beneficiary of the protective innovation in the secessionist Biafra. And this was the manufacture of military hard helmets. A pre-war experience that aided "Uzummuo" and his aides was their previous familiarity with the quality and handling of metal sheets. Remembering that sheet metals were both hard and somewhat pliable made them possible candidates for inputs. In their underground workshop, the group designed cardboard patterns which when curved or folded carefully would produce paper helmets of various sizes for human heads. With the above success, they unfolded these paper helmets, used scribers to get their profiles on the sheet metals, and used shears to cut permanent templets for helmets.

First, holes of the desired sizes of the hard helmets were made on table-like steel sheets 2' × 2' × 2''. Then, half moonlike bowls of cast iron were welded to the steel table in such a way as to receive whatever was dropped from the hole at the top of the table. Thirdly, press machines with human-head-shaped cast iron of various sizes were placed directly above the half moon-like bowls.

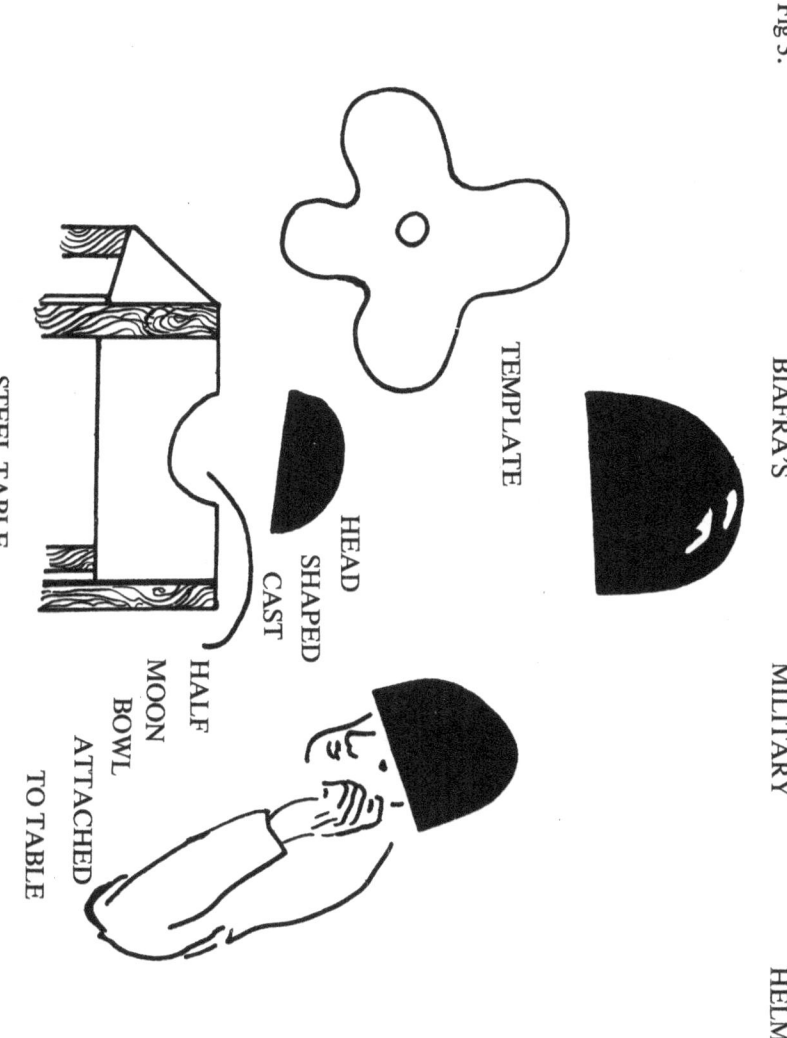

Fig 3. BIAFRA'S MILITARY HELMET

As soon as the steel pattern from the templet was placed in any of the bowls, the hydraulic press with the human-head-shaped cast iron is gradually lowered. As it gradually entered the bowl, the sheet metal pattern slowly folded and the ultimate result was the production of the Biafran military steel helmet. Figure 3 shows one such helmet.

The economic significance of this Biafran war innovation is that cheaply produced steel hard helmets are needed in construction business in present Nigeria. The production is not very demanding and can therefore be good investment for small scale artisans.

vii. *Rockets*

Many statements and otherwise, indicated tangentially that many Biafran civilians, miles away from the theatres of war, lost their lives from the Federal Nigerian Army's rockets. Partisan Biafran historical analysis of the civil war claim that such deaths occurred mostly in market places, churches, refugee camps and hospitals. This study considers a statement just like the last one as a means to whip-up sentiments favourable to the secessionist Biafra. Nevertheless, rocketing from the Federal side occurred in Biafra. In a war in which the secessionists were bitter, if not anything, the occurrence created the urge to retaliate. But retaliation by desire was easy. Retaliation with actual rockets was not easy at all in early Biafra.

The ambition for retaliation by the secessionists though, had two factors in its favour. The first was a pre-civil war knowledge of the manufacture of local fire-works, fire crackers, carbide works, and explosives (Cervenka, 1971)[12]. Secondly, the secessionists had access, unfortunately, to certain federally fired but unspent rockets (Madiebo, 1980)[13].

Given the above two favourable conditions, the secessionist government set "Uzummuo" and his crew to work. By carefully cutting open and studying the contents of the three compartments of their captured Nigerian rockets, the group got the knowledge of what to do to replicate the rocket. First the two halves of a hollow rocket were produced with clay. From these models, many casts of rockets were produced. Having filled the middle compartment of each piece of cast with explosives and shrapnels, and having attached a half of the cone-like warhead to the front of each half of the cast, the two pieces were welded together and finished by attaching the vane-like tail to the end or rear for control and balance while the rocket is in motion. figure 4 is a specimen.

It has to be pointed out that the rationale for compact packing of explosives and shrapnels in the combustion chamber was to create hot air, ready to generate commotion on the least disturbance at the tail launching point. Generally or as has been the case with other Biafran innovations, the rockets

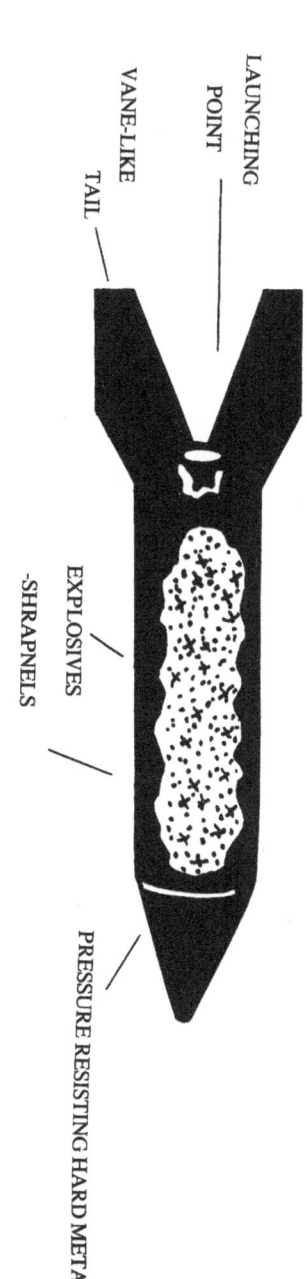

Fig 4. BIAFRA'S ROCKET

were small short-range rockets of about 18" long by about 3" in diameter capable of effective use only with the enemy's tanks in sight or with visible concentration of the enemy. To fire the rocket, the innovating group constructed a tripod, equipped it with a hollow for the rocket to slide through, and raised its front to a certain angle above the ground to help give the rocket a sense of direction when fired. Hitting the hollow at the rear of the rocket as the latter is on the launching pad set the keg of explosives in the combustion chamber into action as the rocket was thrust forward. The gas in the combustion chamber produced by the explosives in trying to escape caused agitation and still more forward thrust or motion, till the hard metal war-head, on hitting its target, encountered resistance. The struggle between the two forces led to the explosion of the rocket, thereby releasing the explosives and shrapnels to do some damage on their target.

Cervenka (1971)[14] mentioned one use of the crude Biafran homemade rockets. As an over-zealous Biafran soldier saw the Federal Army's Russian Mig flying by, he stupidly fired one such rocket at the Mig. The rocket being a short-ranged one could not even get a quarter way to it even though the Mig was flying as low as 2,000 m above the ground over secessionist Biafra. The rocket did one thing certain. It alerted and annoyed the pilots of the Mig who turned rounded, descended to a height of about 1,000 m and rained their 45 mm machine guns with deadly accuracy to smash the rocket source and silence the zealous Biafran soldier for ever.

viii. *Mines*

Perhaps the least disputable area of mechanical innovation for the Biafran group was in the production of various types of mines. One factor that made success possible in this area was that the team of innovators were people who had had experience in operating crude equipments in the past. Certain of them had worked in Enugu coal mines and with construction companies where mines were used. Their productions included mines known as "the Biafran Beer," "the Footcutter," "the coffin," "the Ojukwu's Bucket," and "the Flying Ogbunigwe." For want of time and in order not to make the work appear repetitious, this work has selected the above mentioned ones from a host of mines produced for analysis.

a. *The Biafran Beer*: The first type of mine that the secessionist Biafran innovative group produced was the "Biafran Beer." One thing cynical about naming this mine is that it was a beer to be thrown to the enemy to drink and die. As was previously inferred, certain members must have got their experience of the working of the mine either as coal mine employees or those of foreign construction companies who own quarries. The "Biafran Beer"

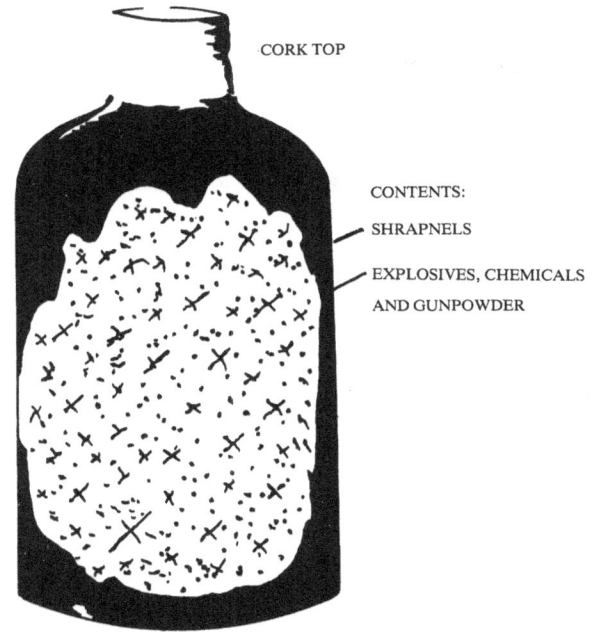

Fig 5.   BIAFRA'S BEER BOTTLE

was a bottle filled with explosives, chemicals, shrapnels, and gun-powder before being tightly corked. A soldier had to agitate and throw "the beer" at an enemy on sight within throwing range. As the resistance of the impact on which it fell broke the bottle, the released explosives and liquid chemicals might catch fire while the shrapnels would hurt the enemy. Figure 5 shows its specimen. Like many other Biafran innovations aforementioned, "the Beer" had the disadvantage of being a low-range weapon. Many users were detected and machine-gunned to death before they had the opportunity to throw them at the enemy. Furthermore, one cannot rule out the possibilities of unspent "Beer." Though this is an innovation one can say and rightly so that this innovation, helped the Biafran soldiers to kill themselves. The author wonders the sense of trying to fight a lion "the Federal Nigerian Army" with an empty hand. Despite these weaknesses and criticisms the secessionist Biafra claimed a pride of its innovation. Without speculating on its economic significance the author holds the opinion that it has a remote economic significance, if it has any at all.

b. *The Footcutter*: The weakness of the "Beer" was realized shortly after its innovation. Hence "Uzummuo" and his group began to tinker with local cannons. It has to be pointed out that cannon firing has been a common practice in southern Nigeria and mostly in the secessionist area during funeral ceremonies. The idea which the innovating group hatched was how to modify cannons as weapons of war. What the group came up with was "the Footcutter." Rudimentary, it consisted of gun powder, explosives, shrapnels and filled t-pipes driven into the ground so that the t-handle pointed towards an on-coming enemy. Reminiscent of its name, the height of the t is about knee high. Being linked together with a line of gun powder, these pipes were set ablaze as the Nigerian infantry got within range. The "footcutter" would cut their feet indeed. The weakness of the footcutter was that while the advance guards of the infantry may be hurt, the rear guards of the infantry were never hurt; so the latter usually dealt machine-gun blows on everything that lived around the source of the footcutter. It may be better to point out that it would be foolish to expect any economic significance of the "footcutter" beneficial to Nigeria except as a war tool. Even as a war tool it is a very poor and low key one. Figure 6 shows the footcutter.

c. *The Coffin*: Reminiscent of the fact that so many Biafrans had been claimed to have died by the secessionist from the Federal Army's shelling, even though their assertions had no solid basis, the next mine that was innovated by the ghost innovator was "the coffin." As the name indicates, this mine resembled a coffin, always as long as the width of an existing main

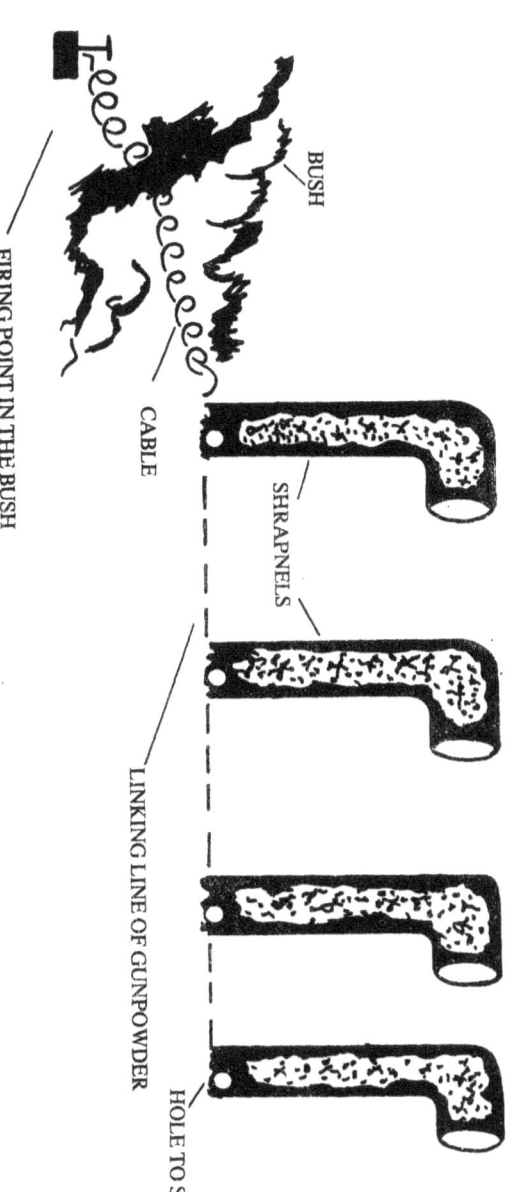

Fig 6. BIAFRA'S FOOTCUTTER

road. It killed people to be put in coffins. Its constituents were a coffin-like metal box, cast iron, lead balls, shrapnels, explosives, broken bottles, nails, and rockets such as were captured from the Federal Army at Abagana. The coffin was generally buried across the road; and in doing so, it was tilted at such an angle that it would face an on-coming enemy. Boys generally regarded as members of "the suicide squad" were assigned to detonate the coffin at the sight of the enemy by holding the long positive and negative cable links from the coffin together and touching them to the head and bottom of a torch battery. The implication of suicide is that the detonator may also be killed. For this reason this innovation is not much to be credited.

The above secession war strategy has also evoked preventive and detective strategies on the Nigerian Federal Army. Being made smarter by knowledge of the havoc of the coffin, and determined not to die, the Nigerian troops invented an ingenious device to detonate the coffin before the troops arrived. It entailed the leashing of a team of cattle together and sending them as advance troops. Frightened boys of the secessionist suicide squad, on hearing the thumping of the cattle infantry feverishly detonated the coffin though erroneously, only to expose the Biafran soldiers to be mowed to death shortly after. A typical picture of the coffin is presented as Figure 7.

The coffin meanwhile has little or no economic significance to Nigeria and therefore the bases of secessionist Biafra's pride in the innovation cannot be easily seen. The only long-range economic significance which it might have is as a weapon of defense in case of invasion by neighbouring countries. The Chadian-Nigerian disagreement in 1981 and 1983 shows that with further development, such disagreements and invasion should not be ruled out. Being that the inputs of the coffin are local products, the country will not be spending much to settle disagreements.

d. *Ojukwu's Bucket*: The de-factor government of Biafra claimed several innovations like "Ojukwu's Kettle, Tea Cup, and Bucket." However the most sophisticated of this class of mines is the "Bucket." Its chief feature is that it was a cast iron that could rotate up to 360 degrees. Inside the bucket was placed first major explosives like petrol and liquid chemicals. These explosives were put in plastic containers and corked to avoid evaporation. Then a thin cardboard was placed on top of the explosives before dried explosives were put. Finally shrapnels of all kinds were packed before the bucket is corked or sealed off on top. The cast iron must be thick enough to resist pressure long enough for the contents of the bucket to be fully charged. To holes drilled at the lower base of the bucket were attached detonating contrivances which could be used to set off the device by remote control similar to that of the coffin. The narrowness of the base of the bucket was so

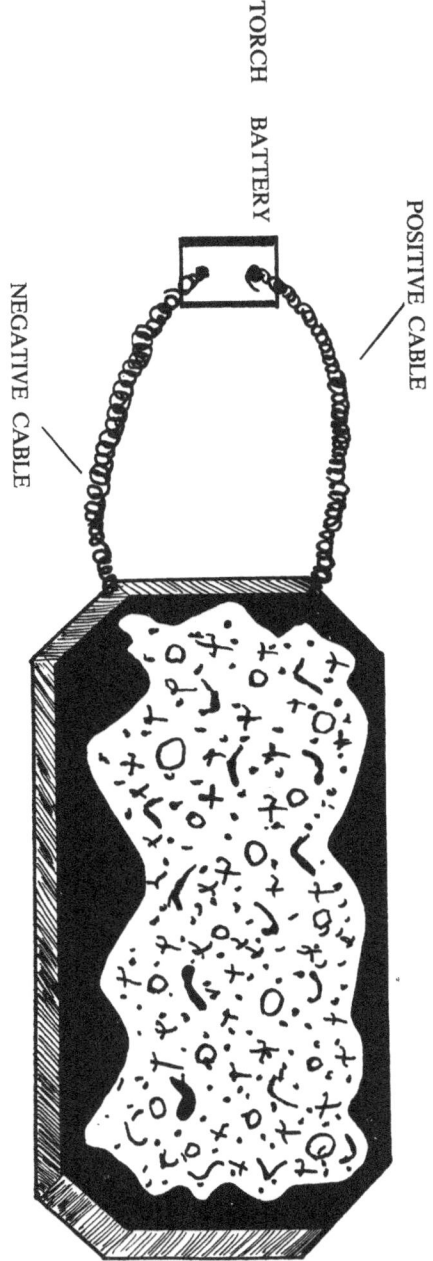

Fig 7.

designed as to generate great commotion among the major explosives and shrapnels, while the bell-shaped form of the bucket helped in directing and concentrating traffic on the target. Furthermore, the ability to rotate the bucket up to 360 degrees made it immaterial as to the direction from which the enemy came, where the bucket was located for launching, and whether advance cattle troops were used or not. However the best mounting position for "Ojukwu's Bucket" was at the side rather than across the road. Being such a wicked device, detonating it anytime never spared many of the enemies. Figure 8 presents a specimen of the "Ojukwu's Bucket."

As a detonating device, this innovation is significant economically to the country. Rather than spend many man days trying to pull down old and dilapidated buildings and bridges, this contrivance can do the job in a matter of seconds and save the labour. Furthermore it has added an additional dimension to the firing power of the Nigerian Army if exploited.

e. *The Flying Ogbunigwe*: The last in the series of mines and the most sophisticated of them all was the flying "Ogbunigwe." "Ogbunigwe," alias the mass killer, really flew. It appears that its flying ability was somewhat exaggerated for it did not fly far enough like the rockets of the technologically advanced countries. Nevertheless, it flew, and the flight was just a few miles from the launching point. The innovation of the flying "Ogbunigwe" came almost too late in the secessionist war; for it came at the tail end of the war. Without going into details, suffice it to say that the ingredients were similar to those of the aforementioned mines. What set it out as unique was its modus operandi. It was usually launched from a launching pad. An eye witness account described it as a huge barrel-like contraption that looked like a medieval siege-gun, but was actually Biafran home-made secret weapon which threw a terrible explosive charge and liquid flame all over the approaching enemy (Ellison, Daily Express, December 10, 1969)[15].

The flying "Ogbunigwe" has a lot of economic significance to Nigeria. If not anything, it can serve as the first step in constructing modern war rockets. This statement may not be acceptable to the technologically advanced countries. However, if a country does not want to be left behind it must start somewhere. And this is the basis for Nigeria. If the research group could be rallied, attractive incentives should be given to them to improve on the research. Or else Nigeria would be left behind.

ix. *The Biafran Shore Battery*

The Federal Nigerian Army had placed a cordon around the land area of secessionist Biafra and blockaded the coastal area; but the stiff-necked secessionist still refused to give up. Even the attrition of its land area and human

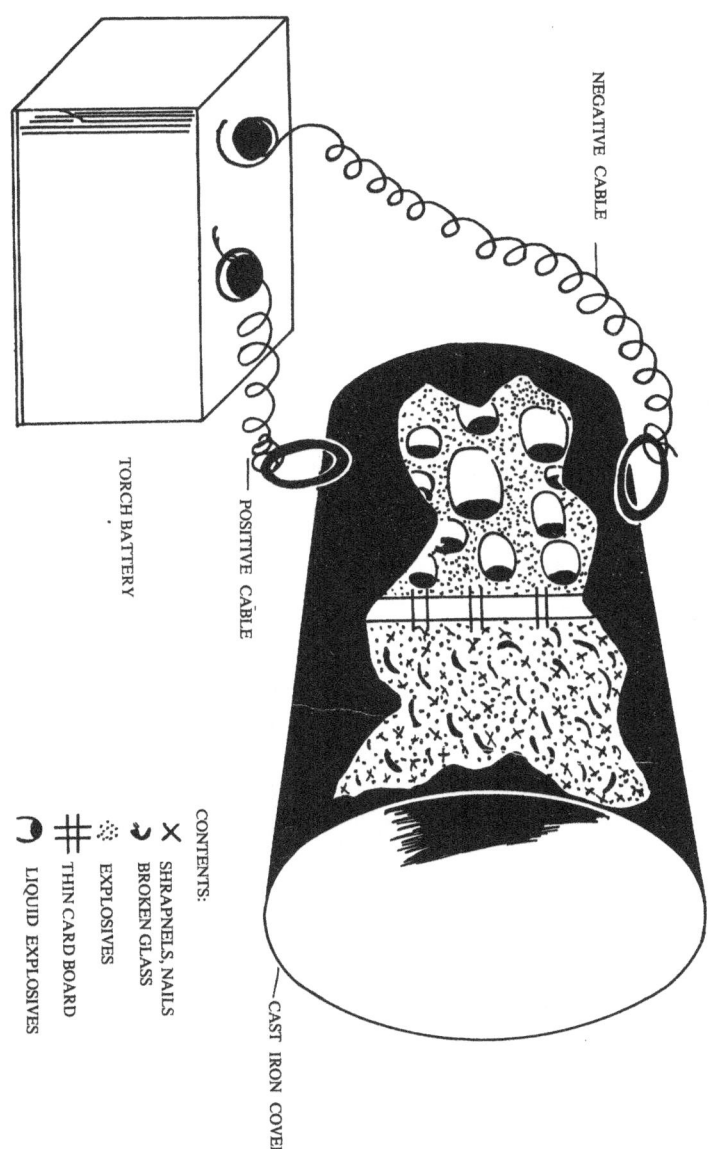

Fig 8. OJUKWU'S BUCKET

sufferings that occurred from the cordon did not compel the Biafran war Council to given up. The Federal Nigerian Army was compelled to adopt a new strategy — attacks on the area by lakes, rivers, and ocean estuaries.

However, in anticipation of river invasion and aware of the vulnerability of Biafra from such an invasion, the Biafran war chief had requested "Uzummuo" and his group to devise a means to foil such an invasion should it occur. What the ghost innovator did seemed to suggest that they knew the Old Testament, of the Egyptians chasing the Israelites out of Egypt and across the Red Sea; and how the Lord instructed Moses to use the Red Sea to stop the Egyptian on-slaught. Could the Lord help him to innovate a device to check the invading Nigerian Army from the estuaries, rivers and lakes?

As this crude Biafran innovator sought for the way out, certain ideas based on daily observations of events began to occur to him. The first was that water poured on burning petrol increases rather than reduce the intensity of the conflagration. Secondly rubber sticks on whatever it touches as it burns. The third is that positively and negatively connected cables to a battery immersed in water shocked when touched. Having toyed with the above ideas for a while the ghost innovator came up with the idea of the "Biafran Shore Battery." The contrivance entailed stuffing connected pipes with petrol, liquid ammonia, carbide, shrapnels, other explosives and ground tyres before sinisterously planting the contrivance across the river. The pipe connection must be well corked to avoid soaking the contents with water. Positive and negative cables linking mechanisms were made to be on the Biafran side of the river. By using a motorcycle battery to connect the positive and negative cables, a force that cause a commotion to the river was produced from the incendiary materials in the connected pipes. Ojukwu (1969)[16] reported one use of such a contrivance as 8 Nigerian Army boats tried to cross from Asaba to Onitsha. It has simply to be speculated that the consequence was likely to be very disasterous. Boats might be sunk and many hands lost, as the river was too wide and fast to be swum.

The shore battery had already been innovated of course. But what significance is it to Nigeria in its bid to develop? It has only the quasi econo-military importance that it can be used to mine its coastal areas and prevent intruders from getting into her waters. It can be said that it also opens up an area for further research.

x. *Armoured Vehicles*: A Federal Nigerian Army monster that always sent the Biafran soldiers fleeing was the former's armoured vehicle. Cutting trenches along the roads and felling trees across the roads have been only temporary checks to the advancement of this monster. Even land mines had been found incapable of stopping its advance. Furthermore, behind its advance followed hoards of the federal infantry which dealt hard blows on the secessionist troops.

As had been usual, the secessionists not only wanted to stop this monster but wanted also to retaliate. Their desires had one factor to their favour. Having noticed that the Armoured cars were slow moving machines, the innovator-in-chief came to the conclusion that the numerous available caterpillar tractors would constitute a good base for innovation. Using the spirit of creativity, self-reliance and crude science in technology which encirclement and war pressure had produced "Uzummuo" led the welders into producing a mass of steel sheets on the wheels. One of their products was the "Biafran Red Devil," an armoured vehicle which suddenly appeared and routed the least expecting Federal Nigerian soldiers at Ore. The machine was abandoned at Ore by the Biafrans in the counter-attack that sent them fleeing for their lives.

Another of such Biafran armoured vehicles was nicknamed "Genocide." It was the product of the Biafran weld-shop in Port Harcourt. "Genocide" provided a challenge to the Federal Army's 106 anti-tank guns and armoured vehicles at Ikem near Nsukka. It was not only a morale booster to the secessionists but also stunned the Federal Army when their anti-tank guns could not easily put it out of action. Though "Genocide" was an innovation worth appreciating, it was plagued with the weaknesses of being so heavy that it could not put in more than ten miles per hour. Consequently, it could not be sent quickly to a point of action. Secondly, being the product of crude innovators, or amateur armour car builders it suffered from constant overheating. To remedy this weakness while in action, it had to stop after every 30 minutes to cool down.

Despite the weaknesses of the above locally made armoured cars, one could rightly say that their innovation was a pointer in the right direction for the Federal Army. If nothing else, it was an eye opener to what Nigeria can do; it was a pointer to possible post-civil war technological capability of Nigeria. Parts from old tractors can be salvaged and be used to produce such equipment rather than import them from abroad. The author is of the opinion that since the imminent of war between Nigeria and her neighbours is somewhat remote, products from such a crude technology are meanwhile adequate. They will offer training grounds for future improvements.

xi. *The Gunboats*

A central point implicit in the analysis of Chapter II is that the secessionists innovations were borne out by the necessities to contain the strategies of the Federal Nigerian Army to suppress them. The anticipated invasions of Bonny, Asanamfor, Onne, and Port Harcourt, all locations accessible by water had led the Biafran military authorities to think of repulsive measures in case they happen. As many of the people around these areas were fishermen good in boat building the defacto government requested cooperation from them in the felling of big trees and the building of large boats out of such tree trunks. The sides of these boats were plated with steel sheets while the tops were covered with roof-like steel sheets. "Uzummuo" and his crew then equipped the boats with Volkswagon car engines to operate them. The sides of the boats were perforated in such a way that the secessionist soldiers could sit inside and fire the Biafran smuggled relatively heavy guns. Madiebo (1980)[17] referred to the use of such home-made gunboats at the battle of Bonny.

The anticipated invasion of Port Harcourt at the early federal assault on the estuaries had stimulated the de-facto military authorities into cannibalizing every usable part from rotten, grounded ships in Bonny, Port Harcourt, and Calabar ports. By re-inforcing the hulks of some of such ships with very strong steel plates, and having equipped them with Biafran home-made weapons, the Biafran innovative group produced the home-built armour-plated warships which in conjunction with the gunboats constituted the nucleus of the much-talked-of Biafran Navy (Madiebo, 1980)[18]. The Navy at the battle of Bonny put up a surprisingly stiff action with the Nigerian Navy, sinking some of the latter. The latter had to go back to the open sea, regrouped, planned strategies, came back, and destroyed the backbone of the secessionist navy.

The technologies of the secessionist production of gunboats and warships have much economic significance to Nigeria. It is a proof that Nigeria can produce modest ships with which it can guard its territorial waters. They will serve as supportive warships for deeper ocean penetration. Secondly, the technologies have shown that many vessels can be build to exploit the abundant sea food in our territorial waters. The coast and rivers of the country are endowed with abundant useful sea food. Finally, the technologies of building such boats and war boats will give abundant employment to many of our high school graduates who otherwise have been incapable of finding employment. They will work in the navy and fishing boats. It is likely that the Federal Government's acceptance of such technologies will still improve the country's technological base in this area.

xii. *Battery Reactivation:*

A war induced innovation, though a minor innovation, was the reactivation of old batteries. The innovation was carried out by a school boy and soon became a household innovation. But it was of great consequence to the secessionists both militarily and otherwise if their contacts were not to be cut off from the outside world. It was the result of a little child playing with an old dying battery. During the play, he illegally made holes at the top of the much valued battery. As the old brother saw this, he tried to snatch the battery off from the child but the battery unfortunately fell into a basin of salt water. The battery was pulled out, sun-dried, and when later on tried was found to perform better than before. This accidental innovation was quickly transmitted to many other boys who collected dead batteries to be used for experimentation. Invariably these batteries became relatively more active. With this confirmation, it soon became news in Biafra that salt added to old batteries through holes at the head made the batteries perform better. Scientifically, the addition of salt entailed the restoration of lost electrolyte in old batteries. It is the chemical reaction between the zinc cover of the batteries and the electrolyte that produced light in the batteries. It has to be pointed out that this innovation was not strictly intended for war purposes. Nevertheless, it was exploited by the army for lighting and communication purposes.

The economic significance of this innovation is that it has set the country on the road to battery production. The Federal Government should clamp down on imports of batteries and encourage the establishment of battery reactivation industry. The war knowledge has shown how reactivation can be done. And the author of this work believes the economy has reached the stage where it can do it. It should be a small scale industry.

xiii. *The Biafran Bush Refinery*:

The need for fuel to supply motive power in an economy that had little or no contact with the outside world was very acute in the secessionist Biafra during the Nigerian civil war. Efforts to satiate the above need led to much tinkering on the part of both the Biafran scientists and many car owners who were very often hard-up with shortages of fuel. De-facto Biafra had one favourable condition to technological innovation in this area. It still retained certain areas where petroleum or oil could be produced. The technique of fuel production by car owners was a back yard innovation that involved few drums and water to cool the fuel. However the more scientific method of production was that innovated by the Research and Production group known as "RAP." According to Professor E. N. Ugochukwu in 1980, a once member of "RAP," their innovation was based on local raw materials.* Their mini or bush refineries produced petrol, kerosine, and diesel of reasonably good quality which with a little more research and experimentation would meet the standards acceptable in other parts of the world. A specimen

---

*Currently professor E. N. Ugochukwu is the Head of Biochemistry Department, University of Benin, Nigeria.

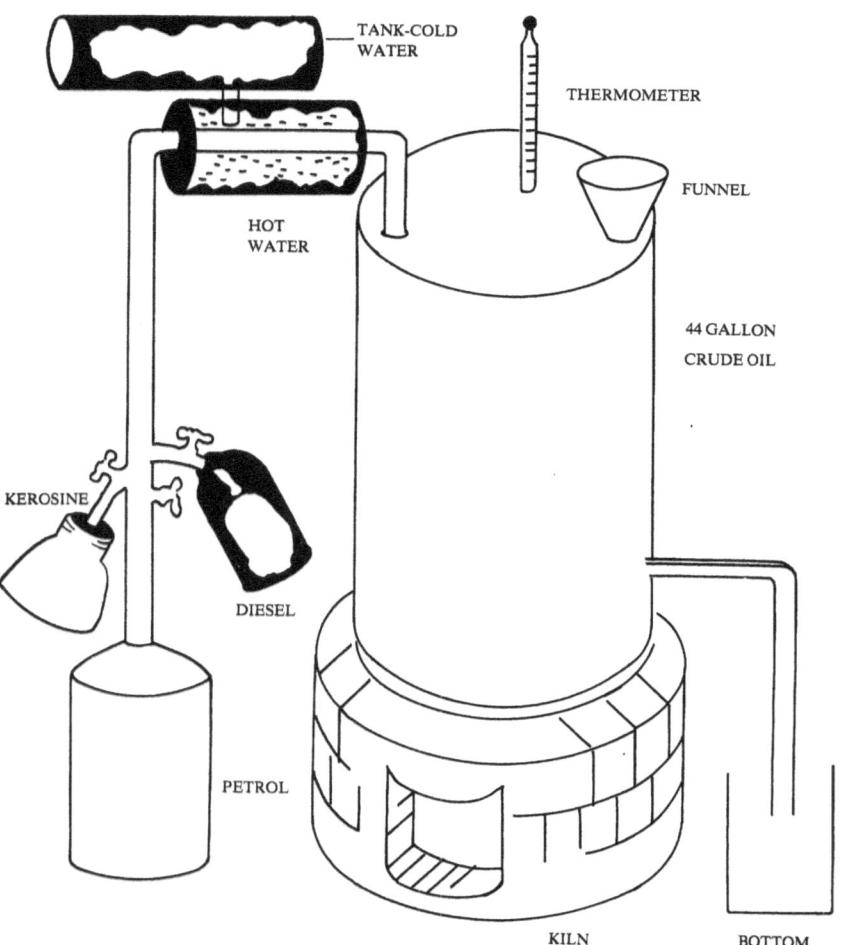

Fig 9. BIAFRAN BUSH REFINERY

of the Biafran Bush Refinery is presented in Figure 9. While only the mechanical aspect of the refinery is presented in this section, the chemistry of fuel production has to be deferred until the treatment of chemically war induced technologies in Biafra.

The economic significance of the Bush Refinery is obvious but will take some time to be attained. Nigeria has scientists who can produce refineries no matter how crude. The unanswered question is why spend limited foreign exchange in purchasing foreign refineries which present problems of spare parts when they break down, in a country where crude alternatives are available? Is it the crudity that scares us out? Is it not likely that with time these crude indigenous refineries would be upgraded? Furthermore, the country has many scientists who would otherwise be working in such refineries but are not. This is a waste of human resources.

B. *BIAFRA'S WAR INDUCED CHEMICAL INNOVATIONS*

A key contention of this Chapter is that belligerency instills in nations the determination for calculated thoughts and action essential to prosecuting and winning wars. For example, it was through calculated thoughts and actions that the Romans of 13th century came up with the idea of a drawbridge with which to keep off their invading enemies out of reach. Similarly, the Viet-Congs had devised the boobytrap with which to fight the more superior American soldiers during the Vietnamese War. The more technologically advanced Americans on their part had calculatingly produced watch-like bombs to get at the picky Viet-Cong soldiers. Implicit in the above examples is a feeling that war and war strategies of opponents lead the other sides to technological innovations not only to meet the needs of war but also business and social needs. If we accept the above examples as having elements of truth, then we shall go on to say that the Federal Nigerian Army's Strategies during the civil war induced secessionist Biafra to indulge in chemical innovations. If this case is positively proved, then it will add to the refutation of the belief and often heard expression that bellicosity is rather a cause of decay rather than a promoter of technological innovations.

Chemistry, we know is a science that deals with the composition and properties of substances, and with the reactions by which substances are produced or converted into other substances. But chemistry as defined above is very advanced, broad, and of little or no interest to the developing though blockaded fighting rebellious Biafra. If we accept the above definition of chemistry, one may not see any technological innovations by the Biafrans. It is therefore the intention of this section of this chapter to have a narrow sense of chemistry which will make this analysis sharper and also include those claimed chemical technological innovations in secessionist Biafra.

The fighting Biafra no doubt wanted chemical innovations that would improve its fighting power. It wanted, therefore, chemical innovations that would help it to detect and determine the quantities and qualities of useful local resources it had. The rationale is that when such knowledge is gained, and applied to useful purposes, it would improve its chance of winning the war. Put in other words, applied chemical technology would not only help her win the war but, also in a situation where war and non-military forces interact and intertwist, promote industry and material welfare of the people. It is from this point of view that the chemical technological innovations to be dealt with in this section of this chapter are broken down into war-power enriching and civilian welfare promoting innovations.

i. *Military Oriented Chemical Innovations*

A fact that should be borne in mind in the analysis of the Nigerian Civil War is that the secessionist Biafra did not get into the war with the intention of winning it militarily. This statement is contingent upon the fact that it was most of the time a defender rather than an aggressor. Its intention was to keep the aggressor at bay till the latter became tired of aggressive action. This was its technique to win world sympathy and possibly recognitions.

Given such a target the secessionist government went only for limited arms that would enable it achieve its desired objective. However, as the pressure from the stronger, more numerous and more powerful Federal Army's strategies increased hardships, the need to still achieve the objective forced the Biafran leaders to call for helps and ideas from the chemical scientists. If one were aware of the meaning of rebellion and the objective of the secessionists, then one would expect much response both from actual scientists and impersonators. Two things were common with these two groups. One is that at one time or another in their school career they had taken chemistry. Another is that each was confident that in one way or another it could throw in an idea that might be helpful. The group gathered in the underground defacto government provided laboratory and as they exchanged views, possible helpful ideas began to crop up.

a. *Explosives*: The first useful idea that the group came up with was how to manufacture an explosive. As research scientists mostly, they exploited their previous knowledge in universities and research institutions in their bid to manufacture explosives. They could still recollect that monovalent radical (OH) group of chemical is generally present in all hydroxides. Two chief sources of this chemical groups easily identifiable in the secessionist area were alcohol, starch and common cotton. They could still recollect the existence of the second group called the nitro group (NO_2), group whose two chief sources were nitric acid and sodium nitrate. Library research revealed to the scientists of the de-factor government that the replacement of the (OH) group by the (NO_2) group would produce an explosive compound. Such an explosive was essential in the manufacture of gun cartridges, mortars, rockets, bombs, handgrenades, gunpowder, and "Ogbunigwe." The explosives that were produced were nitro-products of the various organic compounds such as starch, cotton, glycerine, and toluene.

b. *British Gun Cotton*: A material that was used in the production of explosives by the secessionist Biafran scientists was cotton. Cotton lint, a biological material known as cellulose, was known to consist of a complex carbohydrate strings of glucose endowed with a lot of free (OH) group. According to Dr. H. O. Uwaegbute of the University of Nigeria, Nsukka (1981)*, though cotton was initially used by the secessionist scientists for explosive manufacture, the Federal Army's Strategy of blockade soon made it scarce especially as Biafra was not a cotton producing area. The quest for an alternative led them to the discovery and tapping of kapok or silk cotton as local alternative. Incidentally the silk cotton trees grew abundantly and wildly in this area. Its pre-war use was for stuffing mattresses and pillows.

A prerequisite to using kapok in explosive manufacture was the making of a nitrating mixture, a mixture of fuming nitric acid with concentrated sulphuric acid H_2SO_4. The latter is a heavy corrosive, oily liquid. Into the nitrating mixture was dumped well-ginned kapok while at the same time stirring thoroughly. When the input was thoroughly well mixed, brought out and washed to remove excess acid, drying yielded the yellow looking kapok known as nitrocellulose, or popularly the British gun-cotton. This explosive was found to be stronger than gun powder and consequently the secessionist scientists allowed no naked fire near it. It must be pointed out without going into specifics that many Biafran scientists at the initial stage of the development of the technology were seriously injured. The unlucky ones even lost their lives. However these are among the prices paid usually in the bid to develop a new technology.

In the preceding section that dealt with mechanical technological innovations, it was pointed out that explosives were necessary in the manufacture of cartridges, mortars, grenades, bombs, and "Ogbunigwe." The production of nitro cellulose mentioned above out of local resources quickened secessionist Biafra's arms production. By applying heat according to a specific formula to

*Dr. H. O. Uwaegbute is currently with the University of Nigeria, Nsukka-Nigeria.

both nitrocellulose and nitroglycerin the powder used in arms was produced.

To an unbiased analyst, it appears that the production of the "British Gun Cotton" locally by the secessionists would be economically advantageous to Federal Nigeria especially as local inputs are readily available. The skill is there too. Its local production would stop one of the sources of leakage of scarce foreign exchange. With due recognition that abundant power in the form of cartridges might lead to accidental and malicious shooting of people, it has to be pointed out that plenty of cartridges would satiate the ambition of many double-barrelled gun owners for hunting.

c. *Propellant Powder*: Having attained a reliable base for the production of explosives, the secessionist chemical product innovators went into their business of producing small arms to be used in the war. Chief among their products was the propellant powder used in cartridges, mortars, bombs, and artillery shells. The employment of gel with gunpowder was the principle on which the explosives in the various types of "Ogbunigwe" were designed and produced.

It may be interesting to note that the Biafran chemical scientists innovated local percussion caps used in local guns and the cartridges of double-barrelled guns out of local inputs. These caps were made of mercuric fulminate. The process consisted in dissolving mercury in trithionic acid before precipitation in alcohol took place. The precipitated result was known as mercuric fulminate for fulminating the bottom of gun caps and double barrelled gun cartridges. Though it was pointed out that alcohol was used in the process of precipitation, the chief source of such alcohol was local "*mmanya ngwo*" or palm wine.

As was indicated in sub-section (b) above, nitrated kapok yielded nitrating mixture. The secessionist Biafran scientist innovated a use for the sulphuric acid waste after nitrating. This by-product was collected and stored for reactivating old car batteries or for manufacturing new ones.

Just like the case of British Gun-Cotton, the innovation of the propellant powder has economic significance to Nigeria. It is a source of skill improvement, saver of foreign exchange, and a means to boot indigenous technology.

ii. *Quasi-Military Oriented Chemical Innovations*

Military and non-military demands of the secessionist Biafra were very much intertwined during the civil war. Consequently, certain demands at the time could be classified as either military or non-military depending on the perspective of the analyst. Be that as it may, petroleum which could have been analyzed strictly under Military Chemical Innovations or under Civilian

Oriented Chemical Innovation is treated as a hybrid of the two.

Petroleum was a very essential commodity in the secessionist war. One may not be very wrong in calling it the cause, the dictator of the tempo, and the weapon of the Nigerian civil war. Knowing that military and civilian activities would be paralyzed by shortage of petrol in the secessionist Biafra, the first of strategies that the Federal Nigerian Army used against Biafra was to cut off the latter's supplies of refined fuel such as petrol, kerosine and diesel. One should have expected this modest measure to paralyze the rebel economy. However, what it did was to induce the search for alternative sources within the area. The Biafrans were lucky for some of the Nigerian oil wells were located within their area of control.

1. a. *The Biafran Bush Refinery*: Efficient operation of military and civilian transport and industries was severely hurt by the clamp down on oil supply to secessionist Biafra. To arrest the ugly situation led to the designing and production of the "Bush Refinery" in Biafra. As had been previously indicated, there were several such refineries, certain of them having been referred to as the backyard refineries. But only the "Biafran Bush Refinery" built by the (RAP) group would be analyzed in this work.

The specimen of the Biafran Bush Refinery had been shown already in Figure 9. But before going into the chemical use of the refinery, there is need to say that the scientists who would operate it were chemical scientists who knew only about water distillation. It is not very likely that they had worked in any petroleum refinery as refiners. So if they made any progress, it must be regarded as the result of persistent hard work, ingenuity and imagination. Secondly, one wonders if these scientists knew what they were up to; that they were playing with naked fire. Let us assume that they knew that they were experimenting with a highly inflammable liquid. It might be speculated that it did not matter if they were exposed to such risks and dangers; for the sentiment that prevailed in the secessionist Biafra at that time was that people should die anyway. And to die, one must die honourably. And to die in the experiment of fuel production is one of such honourable deaths. People should therefore not avoid it. On the other hand, the scientist might live and successfully produce a technology for petroleum production. In such a case, he would be included in the list of innovators of petroleum refinery in Biafra. Such had been the position of the innovators of the bush refinery.

A prerequisite to refining petroleum entailed covering the dome shaped drum with thick mud and standing it on a high kiln. At the side of the drum but close to the base of the drum were inserted lead-pipes to conduct the products away from the drum to the receptacles. The products while travelling to the receptacles passed through the zone of a well-designed system of ice-cold water. The latter was necessary to prevent outbreaks of fire. Both Madiebo (1980)[20] and Nwankwo (1972)[21] gave (RAP) the credit of designing and producing the refinery.

Refining began by filling the clay covered 44-gallon drum with viscose crude oil. A large fire was set under the drum standing on a high kiln while the control taps or product exit taps are locked. It has to be remarked that coal from the Udi coal fields were used when the Federal Army had not taken over Enugu. With the loss of Enugu and its coal supplies many of the scientists used their knowledge of blacksmithing in pre-civil war Nigeria to find alternative sources of heat. Being village boys who had operated bellows for the blacksmiths, they knew that hard woods like iroko logs, oil bean tree trunks, velvet tarmarind roots and logs locally known as "icheku" and "acoia barteri" called in local language "araba" could do the job.

b. *Products: Super Petrol, Kerosine, and Diesel*: By careful heating the content of the refinery to a temperature of up to 180^C, the petrol product known as "Super" was produced. At this point, the tap that discharged "Super" product was turned on so that the product had to pass through the well-designed system of ice-cold water to "Super" receptacle. It should be remarked that the Biafran scientists produced petrol at a temperature of less than 120^C. However such a product being of low octane wrecks engines because it does not generate enough propulsive force. A characteristic of an engine using low octane petrol is the knocking or rattling of the engine while in action. An application of heat to still raise the temperature of the content of the drum to between 180^C and 190^C led to the production of kerosine. A still higher temperature of 190^C to 210^C yielded diesel. Though heating above 210^C would yield lubrication oil, the most urgent needs of the blockaded secessionist Biafra were petrol, kerosine and diesel. So acute were their needs that nobody bothered to produce lubricating oil.

A question which might lurk in the minds of the readers of this paper is how, without differential heating, the secessionist scientist knew when to expect petrol, kerosine, and diesel? This problem was solved by placing a thermometer occasionally into the refinery as it functioned. The thermometer was carefully watched and monitorced. As soon as the thermometer temperature ranged between 120^C and 180^C, the tap of the receptacle to collect petrol was opened while those for the bottom, kerosine, and diesel were closed. Between 180^C and 190^C, all taps except that for the kerosine was allowed to run. Above 190^C but below 210^C, only the tap letting out diesel was allowed to run. After collecting the petrol, kerosine, and diesel, only the tap that allowed the "bottom" to escape would be let open so that the bottom might be collected.

It is not easy to doubt the economic significance of the "Bush Refinery" to Nigeria. Even many years after the incentive to innovate, the ghost of its economic import still haunts Nigeria. First and foremost the products of the secessionist "Bush Refinery" — petrol and diesel eased up mobility and transportation problems that plagued the beleaguered Biafra. Though Nigeria of today is not at war, still it suffers from fuel shortages due to poor performance of the established foreign designed refineries. While reactivation of such bush refineries may not solve fully the country's fuel problems, it will help to lessen them. Secondly, there is no doubt at all that shortage of fuel constitutes in the world of today one of the weapons or sanction against noncompliance. The bush refinery was a release from such a noose and could be used by Nigeria when the established refineries are out of order. Though, it might be argued that the products of the "bush refineries" were crude. Nevertheless, upholding the process of their production would provide Nigeria with the knowledge of their weakness and implicitly with ideas on how to improve such products so as to get higher quality products. The latter take time and years of experimentation to produce. Thirdly, many Biafran scientists had pointed out the economic uses to which oil dreggs, known in this work as bottom, could be put. According to them, while petrol and diesel provided the propulsive force in engines and machines, and the kerosine served for both lighting and cooking, the bottom could be mixed with mud for chalking brick and block walls so as to get mould-proof walls, and insect-proof walls. When mixed with clay and coal particles and fired, would produce well baked bricks. It could also be used as pastes for tiles; and when mixed with saw-dust served with saw-dust served for even the "Bush Refinery" or for domestic cooking. In many instances when the bottom is poured on stagnant water, the oil that is left prevented the breeding of mosquitoes. Furthermore when it is mixed with water and the latter product is sprinkled on playgrounds, the product would control the dust. Looking at the above enumerated possible economic benefits revealed by the use of the secessionist "Bush Refinery" one can say that the economic importance of the technology is very obvious. The refinery holds much future for Nigeria though, with many implications and ramifications whose consequences this author does not want to speculate.

2. *Engine Oil.* As one goes through the technology of petroleum refinery in Biafra, one finds that the Biafran scientists did not produce either engine oil or lubricating oil. The dreggs from which these would have been produced were simply wasted. But their failure led despondent Biafran drivers into concocting. This was the practice for which the Biafrans were known even before the civil war erupted. Their ingenious mixing of diesel, grease and light

palm oil did the job. It provided them with a good substitute for engine oil. One could question if their product were good. But the answer to this question is that many engines that used it came out of the war intact. After the war, the concocted products were drained and the engines washed before the normal engine oil was used.

Bearing the above finding in mind, one is safe to claim that the engine oil innovation in secessionist Biafra can help hard-up Nigerian drivers. This is very true in these days of austerity when imported engine oil become more expensive. For this reason, one can also say that the above innovation has not only an economic significance to Nigeria but has also focused on a source of local substitute which would reduce foreign exchange losses. It is an area for more research.

3. *Brake Fluid*. Apart from petroleum refining and engine oil production which the Nigerian Army's strategies had forced on the secessionist Biafrans to innovate, dire needs also drove the Biafran drivers into innovating a substitute to brake-fluid. Unlike the engine oil, the brake fluid was not based on petroleum. Rather it was an accidental and successful matching of things that looked alike. Despondent Biafran drivers noticed that the break fluid looked like coconut milk. And since they could not come by brake-fluid easily, they simply tried coconut fluid as brake fluid and drove off with their cars waiting for adverse consequences (Nwankwo, 1972)[22]. Strangely enough their expectations were not fulfilled. There were no brake failures. The innovation made mobility possible to them.

From the above revelation it can be said that the innovation of the brake fluid has economic significance. But this significance must be qualified. It has significance only to hard-up drivers and to the country during emergency.

iii. *Civilian Welfare Oriented Innovations*

Another area in which the Nigerian Army's War Strategies had affected the rebel Biafrans adversely was in the provision of those chemical needs necessary for civilian welfare. For example, there were deficiencies of chemical food items, animal feed items and industrial inputs. During the civil war, deficiency in the input chemical needs of industries had been very remarkable. Consequently, shortages of industrial products were very common. It seems reasonable to expect that under such a condition the material welfare of the Biafrans was on the decline. To arrest the decline, businessmen who had pre-war experience with foreign firms, like Lever Brothers, and Biafran scientists began to experiment both individually and jointly on applied chemical technological innovations. The end results of their endeavours were the production of several chemically based consumer products. Because the area was blockaded, there was no way of getting foreign inputs for the production system. One should therefore infer from the last statement that such successes as were made were based on locally available raw materials. Furthrmore, being that starvation was a serious problem to the Biafrans, one would expect that food rather than chemical inputs were given high priority in the flights of mercy into Biafra by the Red Cross, Caritas, and the World Council of Churches.

It has to be advised that chemical technological innovations in the context of the advanced countries must not be applied to Biafra. Otherwise one would not see any such innovation. In the context of the developing countries, war has induced many civilian technological innovations, whose achievements the country should be proud of today. The credit for such innovations should go to the indigenes of the beleaguered secessionist economy. Their success arose or can be attributed to the Biafran maxim, "Whoever is rejected by others does not reject himself;" for this reason the indigenes of de-facto Biafra laboured relentlessly to provide their civilian needs. It is not possible to analyze all the ramifications of applied chemical technological innovations made in Biafra during the Civil War. However, by way of exemplification, only a few considered in the opinion of the author to be very revealing would be analyzed.

a. *Distillation of Alcoholic Drinks*: One of the applications of chemical technology in innovation was in the distillation of alcoholic drinks. Certain alcoholic abstainers might be wondering as to the justification for recommending this innovation for creditable mention. Nevertheless, it had been included as a tool for improving material welfare on the ground that by sedation, no matter how temporary, it had made the Biafrans forget their sufferings. That alcohol debilities more than out weigh the sedative temporary reliefs from suffering was immaterial especially during sufferings.

Liquor distillation was not new in the area known as precivil war Biafra. This statement derives from the fact that the pre-war Eastern Nigeria (war-era Biafra) was known to be good in producing *kai-kai, akpateshi, push-me-I-push-you, ogogoro, esilesi*, all various brand names for locally distilled liquor. In fact many riverine villages along the River Niger were known to be good in distilling and drinking such liquor. But such liquor as distilled had one glaring weakness. It was illicit and poorly refined. Being thus poorly refined, it had a high potency of being harmful to health. The war improvements in distillation of liquor in secessionist Biafra made their products no longer illicit and dangerous for human consumption. The distillation being the work of scientists, had a high status, government, industrial, and legal backing. One statement from the ex-Biafrans who tasted it is that it was not very different in taste and proof from some of the imported residual liquor in the blockaded Biafra.

It is very clear that the technology of liquor distillation had been a long time industrial secret. The rationale behind the industrial secrecy is not to set the stage for the destruction of one's market. In other words every distilling industry wants to monopolize the market. This being the case, it cannot be said that the secessionist Biafran scientists and crude local distillers stole the technology from anywhere. One can therefore infer that the secessionist distillers came to it by trial and error.

The pre-requisite for the trial and error was the discontinuation into Biafra of the liquor which people had tasted by the Federal Army's blockade. In the face of the existing need, the recognition of the existence of the need, and the recognition of the existence of the inputs to satisfy the need *"mmanya nkwu and mmanya ngwo,"* that is palm wine and raffia palm wine respectively, people were propelled to try. The people technologically designed and modified available petrol and lubricating oil drums to satisfy the need to produce liquor that suited the local, physical, social, cultural, aesthetic, and economic needs of the war-torn Biafra.

The group that produced liquor that favourably compared with imported liquor in the civil war-torn Biafra was the scientific group known as the Research and Production (RAP). It was the specific section of RAP under Professor Njoku Obi that was credited with producing through distillation the three most favoured brands of the Biafran liquor. It should not be understood that this paper is saying that Professor Njoku Obi's group was the only group distilling liquor in secessionist Biafra. Rather this group has been chosen because of the scientific and uniqueness of its method of production. As had already been pointed out, the principal ingredient was *"mmanya"*, palm wine, and this was allowed to ferment for some days so that a lot of yeast might grow. The production of liquor consisted of three stages of distillation.

The first stage in liquor distillation entailed the employment of a 44 gallon drum and filling it with fermented wine. Distillation began by heating the fermented palm wine in the drum and as should be expected, the product of this stage is called the product of raw distillation. Being raw, it is considered to be possibly harmful and therefore unsuitable for human consumption. It is at this stage that local and unscientific distillers stop. Such products of raw distillation might be equivalent to the illicit gin. The product of the first stage formed a good input for stage two in liquor production. Stage two in liquor production involved taking the product of raw distillation to the laboratory where by the aid of ordinary distillation apparatus, the alcoholic contents of the product of raw distillation are concentrated. It has to be pointed out that the product of this state is still not safe for human consumption. Typical poisonous constituents of the product include traces of methanol, that is a volatile flammable poisonous liquid that consists of carbon, hydrogen, and oxygen, which may cause a form of blindness. It was in the third stage of distillation that the traces of methanol were removed by refluxing. At the end of the third stage, the alcohol produced was as near a pure state as possible. In short, it was devoid of almost all impurities, and therefore, the ripe base for the production or blending of various types of liquor. The base of various types of liquor is alcohol. It is blending that gives each the tang that distinguishes it from the others.

Nature was particularly generous to the Biafran scientists in their blending venture. The war-torn area was endowed with local blending resources in sufficient quantities and varieties to encourage efforts in this direction. In a way, the availability of local resources in a people pressed to the walls stimulated the innovation of an import substitute liquor industry so that the pre-war tastes might be upheld. Among the local resources used to give the liquor the desired tang were spices like ginger, alligator pepper, cinnamon, *"mmeme",* *"uda"* and *"uziza"* to mention but few. One can speculate that these can be used to produce liquor comparable to Gordon Gin, and Silvertop Gin. To produce whisky flavouring and colouring, the Biafran RAP group that undertook liquor distillation experimented with most of the above spices. But the one found most satisfactory was the bark and seeds of *"uda,"* a local cinnamon. The technique entailed immersing the bark and ground *"uda"* seeds in alcohol for extraction of some flavour. By using the flavour, they blended a nice whisky product with very beautiful colour.

Though whisky produced above was no longer plagued with harmful impurities, nevertheless, it might still be dangerous for human consumption because the strength of the alcoholic contents was still indeterminate. To be highly recommended, the alcoholic strength must be specifically known. The formula of lighting the whisky was specifically innovated to do the job. And having determined the alcoholic strength, dilution according to a specific formula yielded whisky that had determinate percentage of alcohol. To make their products conformable, the RAP group used the specific gravity of the alcohol to determine when their product met their acceptable standard. Implicit in the above RAP group findings is the speculation that the inability to measure the alcoholic strength as well as non-refluxing of the pre-civil war liquor in order to remove methanol earned such liquor the not very commendable title "illicit" and therefore unsuitable for human consumption.

Essentially, the first of the three liquor products of RAP during the civil war was *"Chiaka"* alias the secessionist whisky. The meaning of *"Chiaka"* is that God is Great. Le General was the second, and was the popular Biafran brandy. And finally was the Kontrol. The technique of producing Le General was similar to that of *"Chiaka"* except that in the former, the Biafran unique hot scent producing spices known as *"mmeme"* and *"uziza"* were used. Seasonal availability of the above two spieces somewhat restricted their use and Le General production. A General was supposed to be a tough military officer. Because the above liquor gave hot flavour coming from the spices, it was called Le General. *"Mmeme* and *uziza"* were what gave Le General its distinguishing flavour and colour. It was pointed out up above that seasonality of *"mmeme* and *uziza"* affected the production of Le General. Efforts to product the liquor with *"ose oji,"* the alligator pepper produced a poor peppery Le General unlike the type much cherished during the harmattan. The effort to replicate the imported liquor known as Controel resulted in the production of their "Kontrol." The search for its flavouring began with the distilling of the peelings of the orange fruit and ended with the use of tender orange leaves. Consequently, the drink produced the nice orange flavour that is associated with the imported liquor known as Controel. But how did the RAP scientist extract the flavour? It involved estimating a certain weight of young leaves, distilling the leaves in alcohol to extract the flavour, and mixing the product according to a certain formula to produce the secessionist Biafran Kontrol. An additional progress was made in flavouring of Kontrol by concentrating such flavour for future use. A careful consideration of the above liquor production technology has shown that it was borne-out by the pressure from the Federal Army's blockade. It is obvious that without such blockade, the people would not have had difficulties. They would have sat down quietly and drunk imported liquor complacently.

The above technology of liquor production is loaded with several economic implications to the post-civil war Nigeria. One major one is that it has been shown that we can tap our abundant natural resources such as those revealed above to produce various brands of liquor. The possibilities of the above statements is supported by the secessionist achievements. Secondly, the technology exists in all parts of the country, lying dormant, but needs reactivation by the government. Thirdly, the largest industries existing in Nigeria today include the beer industry. It should be observed that every state in the nation has at least one beer brewery, and the greedy states have up to four. The inputs of these liquor are foreign products--a sure source of foreign exchange drain in the country. Therefore, indulging in the secessionist-revealed type of liquor production is likely to improve our understanding of the products still further, not to mention their service as substitutes to imports. Finally, implicit in the secessionist achievement is the fact that no nation has succeeded through eco-technology dependency. Nigeria must find such areas where it has both abundant resources and indigenous technology and begin to experiment for still further progress. The liquor industry provides on such example.

While the economic significance of the secessionist distillation technology has been x-rayed above, it pays to point out certain possible constraint to its consummation. One possible problem to its adoption is the apathy of our leaders, entrepreneurs, and consumers on local products which must be first removed. One who moves about the country tends to find a stigma of inferiority whether genuine or fancied being placed on local products. This shows that we have no pride in our products. We must learn from the Chinese who nationalistically patronized chopsticks, though spoons make for faster eating or the Indians who prefer their national light sari to the heavy warm woolen dresses in American winter. This apathy or apprehension to new things has dampened entrepreneurial zeal. For this reason the psychology of the people, politician, businessmen, and the masses alike must be worked upon. For while the politicians vote for upholding the technology, the businessmen will finance it, and the masses will patronize it. A way to achieve the latter is through advertising and education that such locally made products are not inferior to their imported counterparts. This is the way to remove the stigma of inferiority placed on the locally distilled liquor if adopted. This will make the commodity widely accepted. In addition to all that have been pointed out above it has to be said that such locally distilled liquor must be protected no matter the cost by the Federal Nigerian Government if it were to survive foreign competition.

b. *The Making of Soap*: Another aspect of secessionist technological innovation that was induced by the Federal Nigerian Army's Strategy of blockade was the making of soap for civilian consumption. Records have indicated that soap manufacture existed even in pre-civil war Biafra, for the area like many other parts of Nigeria produced local black soap as well as the soda soap. The latter was notoriously known for burning up the body due to excess sodium hydroxide. In brief, soda soap was not scientifically manufactured. The former, the black soap, on the other hand, often soiled fabrics when not carefully used. An indisputable fact in Nigeria today is that one has to search hard to find people making either the black soap or the soda soap. This is because of the importation of foreign manufactured powder soap.

Though the weaknesses of the above two types of indigenous soap have been mentioned, one considers them very weak demerits. One therefore wonders on what the justification for treating soap making as path-breaking lay in the secessionist Biafra. It lay in the production of a new and different type of soap, the "Noko Magic Washing Powder" soap. The technology was developed by Mr. P. O. Eche of Nkwerre. Noko Magic Washing Powder soap was pathbreaking in that it was not like its predecessor. However, it must be speculated that it had its pedestal for take-off in the black and soda soap. The Biafran Sun (July 3, 1969)[23] reminiscent of J. F. Kennedy's saying, "Ask not what your country can do for you, but what you can do for your country" branded the innovation a new addition to what the civilian entrepreneurs can do to their rebel economy. Indeed Noko Magic Powder soap was an answer to the scarcity of powdered soap in the war-torn Biafra. It was war pressure and blockade induced and therefore was meant to solve these problems. The hardship created on the masses by belligerency was reduced in the form of the availability of the type of soap they wanted and at resonable prices. It helped to render hoarding of the limited available foreign powdered soap in the war-torn area unreasonable.

The main thrust of this innovation is not on the cleaning power of functions of this soap but with the local development of the technology. The work intends to reveal the development of the technology of Noko Magic Washing Powder Soap for possible post-civil war replication. Revealing this may open the eyes for discovery of possible scientific basis for other kinds of soap. One should expect that, like other pre-civil war soaps in the pre-civil war Eastern Nigeria, Noko soap was made by the action of alkali on fats and oils. Having pointed out previously that knowledge of the technology of pre-civil war soap production was a good base to scientific take-off into Noko soap production, it has to be added that the secessionist area had an abundant supply of palm trees and coconut trees which form good sources of both alkali and fats and oil — the indispensable ingredients in soap making. While the red palm fruits and coconut oil provided the requisite fats and oil, the burning, sieving, and leaching of the nut bearing husks and fronds yielded wood-ash solutions which formed the natural sources of potassium carbonate or simply potash. In a technical language applicable in soap making, the solution is known as lye. By boiling and agitating while it boiled the mixture of lye and glycerine obtained from fats and oil, a foamy light yellowish substance collected at the top of the boiling mixture. The yellowish substance was nothing but very soft soap whose performance depended on the appropriate balancing of the mixture of lye and glycerine. It was here that the technology of the pre-civil war soap and that of Noko Magic Washing Powder Soap parted company. Noko's unique technology lay in the fact that the above soft or partly molten soap must be converted into powder. That was what the innovator of Noko Soap did.

The first step in Noko Soap production entailed scooping the foamy light yellowish substance from the boiling mixture. Having scooped off the soft or molten yellowish substance into a container, Noko soap innovator tried his hand at solidification. This was scientifically done by spraying the molten soap with other salts such as sodium carbonate. An improvised spray equipment was a nozzle fixed to the top of a high pipe. As a reaction of the molten soap to a counter-current stream of warm salt injected from the bottom of the pipe, solidification occurred. The solidified soap was collected, powdered, sieved, scented and coloured to possess the unique qualities of Noko Magic Washing Powder.

One can say with a degree of certainty that the technology of making Noko Soap has some significance to post civil-war Nigeria. First of all it is likely that its science would help in producing toilet soap for personal hygiene. Being that such soaps are used for bath, purification with potassium dichromic is necessary before boiling for several days. After the foamy soft and partly molten top had been scooped off and sprayed with sodium carbonate, it must be quickly scented and coloured before being put into moulds or frames to harden. Nature has endowed Nigeria with a lot of flowers, shrubs, and resins that produce scents and colours. When the hardened soap is removed from the frames and cut into desired blocks, stamped, and wrapped as desired, comparable toilet soaps to the imported ones would be produced. Implicit in the above analysis is the feeling or hope that upholding the manufacture of Noko Magic Washing Powder Soap would not only improve Nigeria's technology in soap making but also would reduce foreign exchange leakages due to imports of foreign soap. It will not only improve skill, but would increase employment. Under this condition the abundant natural resources for soap making are likely to be gainfully exploited.

c. *Salt Production*: One more consequence of the Federal Nigerian Army's Strategies on secessionist Biafra was the shortage of the common table salt -- sodium chloride, a very essential ingredient in the diets of mammals including man. That salt was historically imported commercially is attested to by the fact that it was a widely distributed leading item of trade. Its historical importance lay in the fact that the word "salary" deriving from the latin word "salarium," money allotted to a Roman soldier to purchase salt, was coined out of salt. (Encyclopedia Americana Vol. 28). Without going into food seasoning, food preserving, and other industrial functions of the common table salt, this work intends to concentrate on the technology of the common table salt production which the secessionist Biafra did to avoid the decline in the welfare of its subject.

Salt production technology existed in pre-civil war Eastern Nigeria. However, with the proliferation of the more beautiful, granulated, and cheaper imported salt, the indigenes of former Eastern Nigeria gave up the technology. However with the Nigerian Army's Strategy of economic blockade the civilians of secessionist Biafra were quick to reactivate the technology. One effort worthy of mention was that the Biafran scientists carried out experiments to produce salt from many known locally salt-tasting vegetables, shrubs, and roots. This was in keeping with the improvisation attribute of the Biafrans under odd circumstances. It was this attribute that helped to sustain them over the period of the war. One weed which they tried was the Siam weed alias "eupatorium odoratum." This weed, we shall later see, will play a lot of role in protein provision. By burning, sieving, and leaching such weed, salt concentrates were obtained. However, because the concentrates from the source of table salt did not yield sharp and cherished granulated salt, the Biafran scientists turned their attention to salt production from local brine deposits. Two such deposits existed at Ubulu and Okposi, now located in Imo State. As Odumegwu Ojukwu said, the ambition to satisfy Biafran needs led to the refining of local brine found at Ubulu (Ojukwu, 1969)[24].

The pre-civil war indigenous salt in Eastern Nigeria around Ubulu and Okposi was crudely produced. Consequently, it was as hard as rock and less appealing to people. One had to scrape hard to get enough quantity when needed. No wonder why granulated foreign salt was accepted with welcome relief. The need to provide an alternative to the foreign granulated salt blockaded by war, led the Biafran scientists to experiment for better salt than the black and hard local product. The result of their experiment was better in quality and appearance than the pre-civil war type of salt. Being both white and granulated as opposed to the pre-civil war hard and black salt, it must be considered an improvement.

The technology of this war era salt production was based on the scientist's previous knowledge of dehydration in laboratories. It entailed collecting and concentrating brine from either Ubulu or Okposi by boiling. But rather than heat it in an earthen pot to get the crude dark hard blocks of salt as the pre-civil war indigenes did, the scientists fabricated a steel vessel of about $9' \times 6' \times 4'$ from steel sheets. It is well known that corrosion of the sheets by brine could contaminate the salt and render the product as impure as the crude salt; but in the face of war scarcity, who cares very much about the purity? It was indeed luck to have salt no matter how impure. Generally, the brine containing vessel was placed on a high kiln and heating was made underneath. As a result of lengthy heating, dehydration which produced white salt crystals or granules took place. Any lump which might be ungranulated was pounded to get it granulated. The secessionist Biafrans were lucky to have inherited a lot of cellophane materials from abandoned foreign-owned department stores like the U.A.C., and the John Holt Ltd. These were sewn into standard bags by the Biafran girls for bagging and dispatching the salt products.

An additional method based on scientific knowledge of the qualities of caustic soda and hydrochloric acid was also tried. The former is a heat generator, and when mixed with the latter in the right proportion and under ideal conditions generated heat that led to evaporation. The result was the separation of water and salt. It has to be pointed out that this last technique was about to be consummated when the war ended.

That the technologies of salt production developed in secessionist Biafra during the civil war has economic significance for post civil war Nigeria, seems to have some elements of sense. One basis of this statement is that such technologies will help to exploit dormant salt pans at Ubulu and Okposi. Their exploitations are revenue and employment creating in the area. Secondly, it was pointed out that the war era salt products still contained impurities. Efforts would be made to remove them and the result would be an improvement in the country's technology of salt refinement. Finally, if much local production takes place, imported salt may be reduced. The latter will help to improve Nigeria's foreign exchange position.

C. BIAFRAN WAR INDUCED INNOVATIONS — FOOD, FEED, MEDICINE, CLOTHING & SHELTER

The two previous sections have shown the mechanical and chemical efforts the secessionist Biafra had made to protect itself from the Federal Nigerian Army's Strategies. But the war that the secessionists fought was not one which would be fought with mechanical and chemical equipments alone. This statement is contingent upon the new direction of the war as it got prolonged.

A fact that must be borne in mind throughout this work is that the Federal Army was not interested in winning the war at all costs. For this reason, it did not go out for full blow destruction of life and property. All it wanted was to suppress the secessionists. To do this, strategies had to be alternated and occasionally combined. Again in using such strategies, the Federal Army was very wary, lest it might lose the sympathy of the world which it had and by its action helped Biafra to get recognitions. When it became obvious to the Federal Army that all battles are not necessarily won in the battle field where soldiers from both sides die, it relented the use of firing power but strengthened its economic blockade on the secessionist Biafra. One can regard this as closing the loopholes unnecessary to prolonged war. Blockade was a co-operant factor or strategy to the use of military might.

Strengthened economic blockade meant keeping out many imports of basic necessities in secessionist Biafra, especially when the area known as Biafra had suffered a lot of attrition. It could scarcely produce many of its needs. The aspects of this blockade strategy of the Federal Nigerian Army to be dealt with in this section is food, feed, medicine, clothing and shelter. Their restrictions had led to innovations in the secessionist economy. To a certain extent they are basic necessities of life. However, given the tropical nature of Biafra, all of them were not equally important to the Biafrans. The Federal Army, while using all of them, had to give greater weight to the more important ones.

i. *Food*

To avoid problems of understanding, a new concept of food is to be adopted in this study. Food as used here means food for man. It does not include drugs by which to keep them healthy. Food that human beings eat is indispensable to life. It is a source of stamina for fighting. History has yet to tell of a people who fought a war without food. One can say that by adopting this strategy, the Federal Army expected the Biafrans to submit within a short time. However, one thing that the pressure from this strategy did was to stimulate the secessionists into innovating local food alternatives. Though the Biafrans would not accept it, the collapse of their economy was not so much due to military might of the Federal Army as due to the shortages of food. Even the Federal Army would not accept the assertion that it was by starvation rather than by military might that it won the war. While the rib-displaying bodies of the secessionists during the war stood to prove the Biafran objection wrong, documents exist to show that one of the strongest weapons of the Federal Nigerian Army was not military hardware but starvation. Credence to this statement is found in Cervenka's (1971)[25] quote of the German Weekly *Der Stern* of an expression attributed to Major Benjamin Adekunle in August 1968. It said, "I do not want to see any Red Cross, any Caritas, any World Council of Churches, any Pope, any Mission, or any United Nations Delegation. I want to stop every single Ibo being fed as long as these people refuse to capitulate. I do not want this war. But I want to win this war." Cervenka's estimate is that about two million Biafrans died of starvation and more were still dying (1971)[26]. Oyinbo on the other hand using revelations of foreign observers in the then secessionist Biafra estimated a daily death toll of 30,000 (1971)[27]. The foreign observers revelations seemed to be exaggerated and destined to whip up sentiment in favour of the secessionist Biafra; for if we take this seriously, it means that the population of Biafra would be wiped out in one and half years. The figure quoted as the Biafran population at the inception of the civil war was about 14 million. About 11 million people emerged from the war.

It has been pointed out up above that the Nigerian Army used blockade as a strategy against the secessionists. For balanced analysis, it must be pointed out that the Biafrans used hunger and deprivation to arouse th sympathy of the atrocity-hated nations of the world. Proofs to this statement are found in Nigerian Civil War books authored by the then Biafrans. Such books abound with pictures of the starving Biafran children whose ribs could be easily counted. Such books emphasized that kwashiokor an unknown pre-war disease due to malnutrition was the chief killer of thousands of secessionist Biafran children, nursing mothers, and aged people. However, underneath the secessionist calculated action to arouse world sympathy lay hard efforts for innovations in food production and processing. The corner-stone on which these efforts were built was on the doctrine of self reliance. It must be so for the secessionists had no alternative, being surrounded on land by the Federal Army and being blockaded by the Federal Navy.

a. *Food Production Directorate*: As the civil war was not being fought only in the battlefield but also in people's stomachs, certain bold steps must be taken to stave off attacks from this perspective. These bold steps were indispensable precursors to food processing. The first of such steps consisted in forming the secessionist Directorate of Food Production by the Biafran Military Government. The Directorate was charged with the responsibilities of producing or purchasing either through smuggling or otherwise all foods, drinks, and cigarettes first to be distributed to the Biafran Army and then to the civilian population. It was obvious from the function of the Food Production Directorate that it had to produce if production was possible. But where production was not possible it had to purchase and process before distributing. The need to facilitate food production created the urge to acquire and cultivate large tracts of land in the hinterland still beyond the reach of war, coordinate cooperative farming in which farmers were supplied with expert advice, seeds, and fertilizers. One such cooperative farm venture was established at Awka and it specialized in the production of cassava, yams, poultry, and vegetables of various kinds.

b. *The Land Army*: A new innovation analogous to the military was the Land Army. The irony of this nomenclature is that while the military army attacks and shoots people with guns, the land Army attacks lands with hoes so as to plant and produce food. The formation was indispensable, given the rapidly deteriorating food shortage in Biafra. The Land Army by using initiative, resourcefulness, ingenuity, hard work, and trust in God attacked every available piece of land to produce yams, maize, okro, groundnuts, beans, cassava, plantain, coco yams, sweet potatoes, and paw-paw, all ingredients of industrial food processing. In Dr. Imoke's words, the Land Army fights hunger as starvation seemed to be featuring more and more as a subtle weapon of war (Gold, 1970)[28]. Though it cannot be categorically proved, one looking at the post-civil was Operation Feed the nation of the Federal Government would see a lot of similarities. Because the Land Army was a precursor of the latter, it might be possible that the former influenced the latter. Further research in this area is necessary for a conclusive statement.

c. *Research Centres*: Another bold step which the secessionists took to counter the Federal Nigerian Army's Strategy of food shortage was the proliferation of research centres. Be it at it may, research centres are generally known as scrutiny centres. Consequently, the untiring efforts of such centres, the Bende Agricultural Research Centre and Umudike Agricultural Research Station, to mention but few resulted in much success.

The activities or innovations of the research centres were many. One of their achievements was the development of crops for double cropping. Early maturing varieties of crops were their main research inputs. But the most notable developed one was early maturing and equally high yielding rice seedlings. The one developed by Bende Agricultural Research Centre yielded between 3,000-5,000 lbs. per acre (The Biafran Sun, January 16, 1968)[29]. As soon as the seedlings were developed, they were sent to the Land Armies at the riverine areas for quick rice production. One other use of the centres was that they served as demonstration centres to people in close neighbourhood.

The second innovation of the secessionist research centre consequent to war induced protein shortages, known as kwashiokor, was vegetable protein. The two chief ones were "the New Era" and "the Paraguay." These were quick maturing varieties of beans that take less than three months in an ideal soil of well drained sandy loam soil to mature or produce edible fruit. This indeed gave a strong counter-attack to the syndrome of protein deficiency known as kwashiokor (The Biafran Sun, August 8, 1968)[30].

d. *Animal Protein*: Blockade and squeeze of the Federal Nigerian Army led to rapid reduction of animal protein in the rebel economy. Stories had it that what ever goat or sheep that escaped the slaughter of either the rebel civilian or military might, became a victim of the Federal Army. Nevertheless, this story is to be taken as so and does not add anything to the solution of war induced shortages of animal protein in Biafra. What is obvious was that a serious shortage of protein existed in the war-torn Biafra. So bad was it that meat was found only at rich people's tables.

With the growth of fear that the livestock would be completely wiped out by irrational consumers, the Land Army embarked upon three measures. First, apart from encouraging the consumption of snails, frogs, mice, termites, crabs, caterpillars, beetles, and grasshoppers, all formerly pre-war, anathema in most pre-civil war Eastern Nigeria, the raising of rabbits as a quick and cheap substitute to beef was embarked upon. It has to be pointed out that rabbit raising was not popular in pre-war Biafra. The second measure was the encouragement of hatching of eggs and the distribution of chicks to farmers by the more progressive ones. This action can be seen as the rejuvenation of the spirit of oneness and brotherhood consequent to the war pressure. The result of the distribution of chicks by the more progressive farmers was the proliferation of the "hatch and begin your poultry programme" in Biafra. The third step taken to alleviate animal protein deficiency involved the search for protein in certain algae, fungi, leaves, and other microorganisms. One notable success was the extraction of protein from leaves, like those of eupatorium odoratum, alias the Siam weed.

The economic significance of the Food Production Directorate, the Land Army, the Research Centres, and the Search for Increased Animal Protein induced by the war on the Biafrans are obvious in the context of present Nigeria. In the face of rapidly rising population and mounting food import bills there is a need to focus attention more on the resources that exist within the country. The Biafran examples have shown that this can be effectively done.

ii. *Food Processing and Packaging*: One natural problem with most prewar Nigeria as well as the war torn Nigeria, a part of which was Biafra, was the seasonality in food production. For the rest of the country during the civil war, the problem could somewhat be alleviated by imports from out of the country. Blockaded and unrecognized Biafra on the other hand had no recourse. It must do it all alone.

Having undertaken the aforementioned innovations in carbohydrates and proteins productions, it was obvious that the stage had been set for technological innovations in food processing and packaging unless the secessionists were ready to starve to death during the off season in food production. Being encouraged by the visible previous achievements of the Biafran scientists and technicians, several individuals tried their hands at food processing and packaging.

The first effort at food processing was the innovation of what the secessionists branded "the vegetable-rich, anti-kwashiokor salad." Whether this processed food indeed cured kwashiokor or not this study is not in a position to argue. However let us give them credit for their claim. According to Betty Anyakoha*, the ingredients consisted of four wrappings of sliced and slightly fermented oil beans locally called "Ugba" or "Ukpaka " a cigarette cup of fresh local salad fruit known as *"anara"* seeds, about two small bundles of fresh local salad leaves- "leaves of solanium family," two cigarette cups of sliced and dehydrated cassava locally known as *"achi,* or *abacha,* or *jiakpu,*

---

*Betty Anyakoha is currently (1983) with the Department of Vocational Education, University of Nigeria, Nsukka-Nigeria.

or *nsisa*," a pinch of potash, four table-spoons full of palm oil, salt to taste, three table-spoons full of water, half a cigarette cup of dehydrated and powdered shrimps or lobsters, and a teaspoonful of powdered pepper. The technology in preparing the secessionist delight entailed, first washing the local salad fruits and leaves thoroughly in luke-warm water containing a pinch of salt or few drops of milton before draining them in a colander. Secondly, the sliced dehydrated cassava "*achi*" was similarly washed and left in a colander to drain and get soft. The third step consisted in slicing the drained fruits and leaves to reasonable sizes. While the "*achi*" drained, the oil bean wrappings were roasted in the open fire for about five minutes and the grinding of pepper and potash should be mortar done. At the completion of this last step, both the desired measures of water and oil were added to the motar-powdered product while stirring was vigorously done with the addition so as to produce a nice, smooth mixture of orange colour stuff locally called "*ncha*." To "*ncha*" was added salt to taste. The last step lay in putting the now soft sliced cassava, sliced local salad leaves and fruits, roasted oil beans, and powdered shrimps to the "*ncha*" and mixing thoroughly to get the finger licking, saliva-watering, so-called anti-kwashiokor Biafran salad.

The secessionists claimed that the above innovation not only was medicinal in that it helped to fight kwashiokor but also was a promoter of welfare. It was a nice blend of all that the body needed. It was a preferred improvement to the purely carbohydrates formerly considered the essential food of the people. It was to be pointed out that today in the post civil war states that were the secessionist Biafra, people cherish very much the above Biafran war-era innovated salad at high functions.

The second effort in war-time technological innovation in food processing took place at Arochukwu. In the revolutionary venture, an Arochukwu woman successfully preserved a variety of prepared food for ten or more days. Unquestionably, this innovation was remarkable in a humid tropical climate where due to intense heat and high humidity, prepared foods get sour and mouldy few hours after they had been cooked. So revolutionizing was the above innovation that it led to the installation of a new packing factory at Arochukwu by the Calabar Branch of Women Voluntary Service Organization. The above innovation was followed by the development of dry-packing. (The Biafran Sun, November 13, 1968)[31]. The idea of dry-packing derived from the fact that such processed food was sealed in cellophane bags in ration sizes by heating process. As mentioned before, enough cellophane was left by fleeing foreign companies.

Similar progress in food processing technology was noticed in Nnewi at the same time that that of Arochukwu was going on. It may be possible that these two groups exchanged ideas. However there are no proofs to support this speculation. At Nnewi, the Division of Women's Council of Social Services produced 34,718 packs of dry-pack to be distributed to the soldiers in their trenches at Onitsha. The packs were the products of the Council's Dry-Pack kitchen made out of local corn flour, yam, egg, fish, and chicken ingredients (The Biafran Sun, November 28, 1968)[32].

A careful examination of the aforementioned secessionist food process and packaging innovations seem to be indicating that the innovations have reasonable economic significance. The salad is a unique cuisine that appeals to the people of the former secessionist economy. It appeals also to non-Nigerians who have been their guests. Being that the indigenes of Biafra claimed the salad had high nutritive value and flavour, there is a need to test this claim. On the assumption that this claim is proved correct, it will pay Nigeria economically to popularize this dish in her international class hotels. If Chinese foods are served in such hotels in Nigeria, one wonders why this salad cannot be served. The evidence of food pack is too obvious to need mention. Ever since the end of the civil war, states that were once the secessionist Biafra have championed in the production of food packs like chop-one-chop-two, roasted beef and snails, and biscuits. They have set the stage for the post war Nigerian to toe the path as had been done by many advanced countries.

iii. *Animal Feed*

The Federal Army's blockade had not only induced the rebel Biafrans to seek immediate solution to their problem of protein deficiency, but also has compelled them to take a long-range view of the solution to the problem. One can only understand the magnitude of protein deficiency if we accept Henry Jaggi of the Swiss International Communities of Red Cross in Biafra and Dr. Herman Middlekoop, a rural health specialist of the World Council of Churches, findings (Cervenka, 1971)[33]. They indicated there was an urgency to feed eleven million people with mostly proteinous food to the tune of 100 grams per head daily if the population were not to be wiped out.

As by early 1969, protein deficiency had been epitomized in Kwashiokor. The secessionists got it dawned into them that neither the trickle of protein from the relief organizations nor the little smuggled-in from the neighbouring Cameroun could postpone the evil day much longer. It was at this stage that the secessionist government became bent on developing its own local supply sources of animal protein. Being a defacto government devoid of outside recognition, it had no choice but trust in the discovery and development of local initiatives and talents. It welcomed progressive ideas which might have been stimulated by war problems. It has to be pointed out that many secessionist scientists contrived many new techniques to deal with the exigencies or ugly kwashiokor problem.

The sections already treated indicated how the search for sources of protein replenishment had innovated leguminous and aquatic protein sources. It had also been indicated that rabbits were reared to supplement vegetable and marine sources. But apart from rabbits, chickens were found to be the next candidate for quick and easier provisions of animal protein. However on the road to the proliferation of chicken production lay the problem of feed. The latter was in short-supply. The ingredients for its local production were either imported or got from the sea coast which had already been either over-run by the Federal troops or blockaded by the Federal Navy. Efforts at self-sufficiency unsteered by war, led the secessionist scientists under the leadership of Walter Ossai to experiment on feed production with local ingredients.*

The first experiment which Ossai made was to use discarded yam, cassava, cocoyams, and potatoes as inputs. These were known to contain a lot of carbohydrates, an essential ingredient in animal feed. These ingredients were in abundance and at no cost. The intention of research in this area was to spread the results of the findings if favourable, to encourage the "do-it-yourself technique" to the villagers, to retrieve the decadent animal farm industry, and thereby to try to solve the problem of protein deficiency known as kwashiokor. But no sooner had Ossai begun with the above carbohydrate sources than a serious problem cropped up. The problem was that carbohydrates' brans were oval in shapes and as the birds tried to ingest them, they blocked the crops of the chickens, fermented there, and posioned such birds. It led not only to the loss of many birds but also to the search for a better alternative.

Efforts to remedy the ugly situation led to the mixing of rice brans and cassava, with a dash of permanganate of potash being added. This latter innovation definitely was helpful in preventing the death of chickens. Cassava was among the chief food of the secessionists. However, as blockade and war made cassava more precious and starvation more serious, it became a choice between saving the chickens and losing the human population or the other way round. But no sensible person no matter how desperate of chickens would prefer the former to the latter. In other words they preferred hell for the chickens and heaven for the human beings. This problem of cassava shortage stimulated quest in another direction.

It was indicated previously that the scientists of the defacto economy found "eupotorium odoratum" an indispensable source of protein. As this was a

---

*At the time of writing Walter Ossai is with the Poultry Division, University of Benin, Nigeria.

fast growing weed in Nigeria there was no question of its abundance. As a protein source however, it was inferior to chickens. But chickens could not be produced without carbohydrates, cassava and corn, and especially the latter as they were doing in the United States of America. Whatever corn existed in the defacto economy was for human consumption. The search for a substitute was extended to wild tubers, and war induced research led to a stumble over a tuber known as acacia. It was the product of a ubiquitous leguminous trees or shrubs with round white or yellow or purple flower clusters. It appeared that nature endowed the shrub with the above beautiful colours to make it easily attractive and recognizable to man. To reach the tuber, one simply had to pull the shrub up and dig right down below to be blessed with as much tuber as one could carry.

It looked like acacia discovered by the Biafran scientists would prove a highly valued cheap source of the much needed carbohydrates in the animal feed industry. The reason for this last statement is that being a wild shrub, war never restricted its growth. It has to be pointed out that acacia growth could also be found in other parts of Nigeria. But initial attempt to feed poultry and other animals with ground and dehydrated acacia proved disastrous. The reason was that acacia was felt to contain certain unknown toxic material that was poisonous to chickens and other animals. There was hope that with the discovery and removal of the toxicity, acacia product could still serve as an alternative to corn in animal feed manufacture. Analogous to corn-beef, we might be talking in this part of the world of acacia-beef.

An idea that might have helped Ossai and other researchers solve the above problem was the fact that heat breaks down toxicity. So as an alternative to grinding and dehydrating of acacia by dry heat, the wet heat process was tried before dehydration. This consisted in boiling acacia before drying it for use. A test for poisonous material in the product was conducted by allowing a dog lick the resulting water after boiling. No sooner had the dog finished drinking it than it ran round and died. Similarly, chickens fed with such boiled and dehydrated acacia died. Undaunted by the above flaws, and pressured by the blockade-imposed need to be self-sufficient, the secessionist research group continued their quest for the solution of the problem of animal feed. Another idea that might have helped the group was the knowledge that fermentation is the process by which the poisonous elements in cassava could be broken down. Using that knowledge, they boiled and fermented acacia; and to make assurance doubly sure, they boiled and fermented it the second time before dehydrating. Strangely enough, when the product was powdered, it produced granules that resembled those of corn mill. And when fed to animals and poultry, they no longer died disastrously. It could be inferred from the above analysis that it appeared as if Ossai and his research team had innovated acacia tuber both as an alternative and substitute to imported corn in Nigeria's post civil war animal feed industry. Another dimension which the discovery has suggested was the possibility of utilizing the poisonous water from boiled acacia to produce pesticides. If it is possible it will provide a good fight against mosquitoes and cockroaches.

Though acacia was highly helpful in animal feed production, it has to be remembered that it supplied only the carbohydrates component of animal feed. But animal feed contains protein, minerals, and trace minerals besides energy giving carbohydrates. In the bid to provide caged-birds with protein, Ossai and his team collected and burst anthills for the chicks to peck and eat the ants. They also collected, dried, and ground snails. These sources of protein were readily available in the secessionist economy. To provide mineral supplements and vitamins required by birds and animals, the team resorted to one of the discovered qualities of the Siam weed "eupotorium odoratum." Previously, research had shown that it contained 30-34 per cent crude protein as well as a lot of trace minerals and vitamins. Though inconclusive, it was felt that it contained copper sulphate, an essential ingredient used to check chicks diseases. By collecting succulent leaves and stems of Siam weed, grinding them into powder, and sieving the product, the research team produced vitamin supplements which when compared with the left-over from imports in the secessionist area proved to be not different. This discovery led to massive collection of leaves and stems of the siam weeds, washing, pounding, drying, sieving the products, and finally canning and sending the canned products to various animal feel production centres in the then Biafra. By mixing the carbohydrates from acacia with the milled snail or white ant dehydrates, and finally adding the canned product from the Siam weed to the mixture, a balanced meal for animals and birds was produced.

In retrospect, there is no gainsaying the fact that necessity is the mother of both innovation and invention. If the Federal Army's War Strategies had not pushed the secessionists to the walls by both fighting power and economic blockade, Ossai and his team of fellow researchers would have rested on their laurels. The area would have depended on imported feed, and the innovation would not have been made. This innovation has much economic significance to present Nigeria which is very deficient in animal protein. Luckily the local resources are in abundance to manufacture animal feed. If utilized, not only will there occur a poliferation in protein production in the country but also the utilization of the local inputs would serve as substitutes to imported foreign inputs of corn and fish meals. Millions of naira are likely to be saved in foreign exchange. However, one observation worth mentioning is that there have not yet been serious indications that the present Nigeria governments realize the economic implications or significance of the innovation of local inputs in animal feed industry.

iv. *Medicine*

It was implicitly understood that the food shortages which the Federal Army's strategies on Biafra brought with it affected adversely the health of the secessionists. Many people's health debilitated physically, mentally, emotionally and aesthetically. Diseases like kwashiokor, cholera, measles, and malaria to mention but few were rife. However, just as there were individuals and groups of scientists determined to solve food, feed, and weapon problems during the civil war in Biafra, certain others were bent on making technological innovations which were expected to help cure the war era diseases. Analogous to the war of bullets, the innovators of drugs in the rebel Biafra were waging a war against diseases. One of the supposedly innovations made in Biafra during the civil war to arrest the rampant outbreak of cholera was the production of anti-cholera vaccine claimed by Professor Njoku Obi.* The latter asserted that the drug was tested and found very effective. Suffice it to say that since the opinion of Njoku Obi has prevailed in the secessionist area during the war, we gave him credit for innovation, but with the proviso that such credit would be removed if later research proves him doubtful. Meanwhile, this claim is a pointer to an area for further research; an important research in an area with a lot of malarial mosquitoes.

One factor that helped innovation in the area of drugs was the nurturing of the myth that God who gave them the will power to secede would never forsake them. He will give them will power to plod through odds no matter how irksome. With this belief the Biafrans came to the conclusion that every attractive shrubs and herbs were meant to help them medicinally. Consequently, they tried to find solutions to their problems in their beautiful environment. Given the in-ward looking trend which the pressure infused into them, the Biafrans resorted to growing and consuming of priority vegetables like "anala" solanium leaves and seeds, pumpkin leaves and fruit, and waterleaves "telfiaria," all these are highly rated sources of vitamins. The nutrients from these vegetables provided for the delicate needs of the nerves, endocrine organs, and the body system. It was in the quest for solutions to the problems of vitamin deficiency that the Biafran scientists discovered that the hitherto neglected and very common cassava leaves were very promising sources of vitamins especially when the leaves were taken from three month-old cassava.

The syndrome of protein deficiency in man known as kwashiokor, had been aforementioned, as having generated series of research in protein pro-

----

*At the period of writing (1982) Professor Njoku Obi is with the Department of Microbiology, University of Nigeria, Nsukka-Nigeria.

duction. As a result of the search for the solution of protein deficiency in "eupotorium odoratum," the Siam Weed, it was discovered as a by-product that the weed contained a high level of vitamins too. Other discovered sources of vitamins apart from Siam Weed, cassava leaves, solanium leaves, pumpkin leaves, and waterleaves were maize and corn leaves, pepper leaves, *"okazi,"* *"utazi,"* *"achala"* or elephant grass shoots, and velvet tamarind shoots. Certain of these were later dehydrated and stored in water-tight or humidity proof containers for later use as sources of vitamins to be added to carbohydrates.

The economic significance of these innovations are very obvious. They lend credence to what our herbalists had been claiming all along. They are indications to the fact that the drugs we need are at our door steps. Their use will save the country millions of naira on imports of foreign manufactured drugs. However, to make sure that their economic significance is really what they claim to be, there should be more meticulous research in these drugs and vitamins sources. Such a research will improve the country's skill in drug manufacture.

v. *Clothing*:

It was pointed out at the early part of this section on food, feed, medicine, clothing and shelter that clothing was not considered a very strong pressure weapon to use to force the secessionist Biafrans on their knees. This is because the rebel economy enjoyed a tropical climate. Nature is usually very generous in such a climate. Documentations exist to testify that many Biafran soldiers fought bare-bodied and barefooted. However, the Biafran soldiers wanted to be distinguished from the civilians, like is possible with the soldiers of the Federal Army from the civilians. It was to this end that the secessionist Government made a limited number of innovations in army uniforms.

One innovation in this area was the production of "Kampala," a uniform reminiscent of the peace mission to Kampala in Uganda. This army uniform was made out of unbleached calico or baft. By using local chemicals to dye it, the popular camouflage Biafran army uniform was produced. Similarly, the Biafran "Castro" style cap, which with its rising sun badge, became the most coveted and prized war souvenir was designed and produced. Rumour had it that the cap was a secret trade commodity between the Nigerian and the Biafran soldiers at certain sectors of the war, especially when their respective senior officers were away from the battle fronts (Oyinbo, 1971)[34]. the implication of this trade is that it dawned to the soldiers of both sides that they were brothers and should not go on killing themselves. Moreover, if the senior officers wanted to fight they could do so. Other achievements in this area include the production of sandals out of old tyres so that the feet of the

Biafran soldiers might be protected from jiggers and foot-cuts.

vi *Shelter*

One more area in which the strategies of the Federal Nigerian Army had induced innovations was in shelter construction. It has to be pointed out that the need to provide landing and take-off strips for flights to mercy into Biafra had compelled the secessionist engineers to convert a stretch of mainroad into a landing strip at Uli. To protect such planes from the devastating bombings of the Russian Migs, an underground garage was constructed by the secessionist engineers in close neighbourhood. Furthermore, the engineers had used local resources and ingenuity to harness new resources. They broke new fields in using indigenous raw materials to put up modern buildings. The above assertions were proved right by the achievements of the Industrial Era Development Company. The latter consisting of local engineers built an ultra-modern house from the floor to the roof out of local inputs. The building had granolithic flooring to replace imported marble chippings, terrazo, and tiles.

There is every reason to believe that the above war era innovations has economic significance to Nigeria especially in these days of rising costs of foreign building materials. As our local resources make good inputs, they can be good substitutes that reduce loss of foreign exchange to the country.

Conclusion

In retrospect, one who looks at the achievements of the secessionists consequent to the Federal Army's Strategies would no doubt come out with the conclusion that the Biafrans have made some significant forward strides in innovations that would benefit the country. It was unfortunate that the war was fought and many sane Nigerians wish that such should never occur again. However, out of the one that was fought tangential or otherwise traces of mechanical, chemical, food, feed, medicinal, clothing and shelter innovations were visible. What has made such innovations important is that they were all based on local inputs. It looks like the stage for technological progress of the country had been set. Many pessimists may not believe this assertion because they are not very obvious or crystal clear. It is the intention of the next chapter to trace the linkages of such innovations in the post civil war Nigerian economy.

References

1. Alexander A. Madiebo, *The Nigerian Revolution and the Biafran War,* (Enugu, Nigeria: Fourth Dimension Publishing Company Ltd., 1980), pp. 222-24.
2. F. C. Lane, "Economic Consequences of Organized Violence," *Journal of Economic History* XVIII (1958), p. 402.
3. Alexander A. Madiebo, 1980, p. 392.
4. Zdenek Cervenka, *The Nigerian Civil War* 1969-70 (Frankfurt am Main: Bernard & Graefe Verlag Fur Wehrwesen, 1971), pp. 280-1.
5. *The Biafran Sun* Aba, Biafra 1968-1969.
6. *Markpress Release* Aba, Biafra: February 29, 1968.
7. Alexander A. Madiebo, 1980, pp. 35-351.
8. Zdenek Cervenka 1971, p. 315.
9. Chukwuemeka Odumegwu Ojukwu, *Biafra: Selected Speeches with Journals of Events* (New York: Harper and Row Publishers, 1969), p. 341.
10. Alexander A. Madiebo, 1971, pp. 221-222.
11. *Markpress Release* Aba, Biafra: February 6, 1968.
12. Zdenek Cervenka, 1971, p. 315.
13. Alexander A. Madiebo, 1980 p. 225.
14. Zedenek Cervenka, 1971 pp. 140-141.
15. John Ellison, *Daily Express,* London December 10, 1969.
16. Chukwuemeka Odumegwu Ojukwu, 1969, p. 246.
17. Alexander A. Madiebo, 1980 p. 243.
18. ibid, p. 244.
19. American International, *Encyclopedia Americana* Vol 28, (Danbury, Connecticut: American International Headquarters, 1978), p. 161.
20. Alexander A. Madiebo, 1980, pp. 114-115.
21. Arthur A. Nwankwo Nigeria: *The Challenge of Biafra* (Enugu, Nigeria: Fourth Dimension Publishing Company Ltd., 1972), pp. 28-29.
22. Ibid. p. 30.
23. *The Biafran Sun* Aba, Biafra: July 3, 1969.
24. Chukwuemeka Odumegwu Ojukwu, 1969, p. 218.
25. Zdenek Cervenka 1971, p. 73.
26. Ibid. p. 153.
27. John Oyinbo, *Nigeria: Crisis and Beyond* (London: Charles Knight and Company Ltd., 1971), p. 90.
28. Herbert Gold, *Biafra Goodbye* (San Francisco, U.S.A.: Townwindow Press, 1970), pp. 14-15.
29. *The Biafran Sun,* Aba, Biafra, January 16, 1968.
30. *The Biafran Sun,* Aba, Biafra, August 8, 1968.
31. *The Biafran Sun,* Aba, Biafra, November 13, 1968.
32. *The Biafran Sun,* Aba, Biafra, November 28, 1968.
33. Zdenek Cervenka 1971, p. 153.
34. John Oyinbo 1971, p. 87.

CHAPTER IV

LINKAGES OF BIAFRAN TECHNOLOGICAL INNOVATIONS IN POST CIVIL WAR NIGERIA: A SEARCH

History has revealed that Nigeria passed through a period of gruesome fighting for almost three long years between the secessionists known as Biafra and the Federal Army. What has been baffling as one reads the history of the civil war was how Biafra, blockaded and unrecognized, managed to sustain fighting for the length of period that it lasted. Chapter III of this work has attributed the tenacity of the secessionist Biafrans to the war induced rediscovery of indigenous technologies in the area. The proliferation of foreign technologies into pre-war Nigeria made the indigenous technologies to be relegated to the background. The blockade and other war strategies of the Federal Nigerian Army left the secessionists no choice but to exhume and refine their almost decadent indigenous technologies. The approach which the chapter used to reveal the existence of these technologies was both direct and tangential. Accepting such revelations, it is the intention of this chapter to search for possible linkages between the Biafran claimed technological achievements of Chapter III and Nigeria's post civil-war bid to progress technologically. Put in a nutshell, has the post civil-war Nigeria learnt any lesson with regards to technological development from the secessionist Biafra? It is in search of the answer to the above question that this chapter is all about.

One characteristic of the secessionists which must be looked for in the trace for such technological linkages, is whether the post civil war Nigeria has the spirit of resilience, susceptibility to accept, fashion, and replicate the type which existed in secessionist Biafra during the war. For one thing, the secessionists were very good at replicating foreign manufacturers with indigenous resources. Their products were crude, but nevertheless they did the jobs for which they were produced. Another characteristic is quick recognition of emergency. Be it due to war or otherwise, the Biafrans recognized emergencies in time and planned not only for their immediate solutions but for their long-run solutions. One who went through Chapter III carefully would find that with the eruption of the civil war and consequent blockade and hardships, the Biafrans exhumed their dormant indigenous technologies, made so by the proliferation of cheap foreign manufactured goods. They are technologies borne out by hardships and would last long. The new thinking among the have-not nations is that this is likely to be the sure road to development of technology in developing economies.

A prerequisite to tracing possible linkages is to realize that there had occurred two distinct types of government in Nigeria since the end of the civil war. These are the Federal Military Government and the Federal Civilian government. The acceptance of each, of the claimed Biafran technological innovations depends on the type and perspective of each of these Governments. An additional basis of the search for the linkages is a careful examination of the Military and post-Military Governments' National Development Plans, their Progress Reports, and the Outline of the 1981-85 Fourth National Development Plan.

i. *The Federal Military Government Period 1970-1979*

The civil war ended abruptly in early 1970 and was followed by honest-statement of Major General Yakubu Gowon of "No Victor, No Vanquished" (Aniagolu, 1982)[1]. General Gowon looked at the war as a brotherly brawl. It was a brawl that ironically was a blessing in that it offered the country an opportunity to search within herself, test and confirm her existing but almost decadent technological capabilities. Given such a perspective of the war, one expects to find linkages of so-claimed Biafran war era technological innovations in the post war Military Administration. However, it must be stated that no wholesale acceptance of such technologies should be expected at the initial return to peace when the wounds were still fresh and feelings still bitter. The military had passed through ugly military, psychological, and physical brunts. Wholesale acceptance would mean giving Biafra credit for secession. And the Military was not ready for that.

While we accuse the Federal Military government of lack of wholesale acceptance of Biafra's war era technological innovations, we must give the ex-Biafran scientists and innovators their due share of blame for not fostering the linkages. Many of them were afraid of victimizations or retributions from the Federal Army. Hence they did not come out openly to show what they could do few years after hostilities.

Implicit in the above two paragraphs is the fact that the military recognized that the secessionist Biafra made significant technological innovations during the war. But the technologies they chose to accept were non-military rather than military. One indication of the linkage of Biafra's technologies with post civil war Military Administration was the contact, credit, and financial support which the Military Governments gave to Product Development Agency, an indigenous technologically biased development agency based at Enugu, once the capital of Biafra. It cannot be proved that certain of this Agency workers helped to make technological innovations in Biafra during the civil war. But it can be speculated that they did. The essential fact is that during the Military post civil-war administration, the moral and financial supports or encouragements received by the Agency seemed to have borne good dividends. During this period the Agency produced mechanized gari processing machines, kerosine hatcheries, kerosine ovens, and science equipments from local resources, all for civilian use. An Agency like the one above is a "Centre of Excellence" (Animalu, 1979)[2] and credit should be given to the Federal Military Government for using it to promote technological assimilation of Biafra's civilian benefit-oriented war-time technologies. But the Federal Military Government should be blamed for not exploiting other similar civilian technologies possible in other institutes of ex-Biafra.

Another linkage of Biafra's war time technologies existing in the post civil-war Military Administration is found in the latter's adoption of Operation Feed the Nation. A careful study of Operation Feed the Nation seems to show that it is a progeny of the Biafran Land Army. It is a civilian welfare oriented technology and had to be adopted. Like its precursor, it entailed the application of simple indigenous technologies in agricultural development. Once such a knowledge was gained, it was diffused and taught to Nigerians in all parts of the country irrespective of professions. The result of the imbibement by the civilians during the post civil-war Military Administration of the quasi Land Army technology, in the name of Operation Feed the Nation, resulted in the proliferation of backyard gardens, orchards, and family poultry farms all over Nigeria in a manner and tempo, the type of which had never been experienced in precivil war annals of the country. Being that nature is very indiscriminate between the secessionist's agricultural technological innovations and non-secessionist's agricultural technological innovations, the above assimilated technological innovations bore good dividends to the post civil-war Military Administration. There occurred a spectacular increase in food production with consequent plummeting food prices in the early post civil-war years. The technology was a pride booster to the Federal Military Administration. To the common man, it was obvious that the technological assimilation had improved the health and well-being of the Nigerians, not to mention its potency for reducing the country's import bills in food items.

The third possible Biafran technological innovation traceable in the post civil-war Military Administration hinged on the concept of Self-Reliance. This concept was synonymous with what the Biafrans thought and saw to be Biafra. It had dawned on the Federal Military Administration that inward search rather than outward search was the best route to technological advance. The Biafran case had proved it. However where the Federal Military Administration went out of track was in the interpretation of self-reliance.

Apart from the above civilian oriented Biafran technological innovations, obvious and tangential bases exist to support the assertion that the Federal Military Administration of the post civil-war was apprehensive in assimilating other aspects of Biafra's war era technological achievements. One must excuse or even not blame the Federal Military Administration because a good majority of the secessionist technological innovations were not such that would arouse much assimilative enthusiasm among the Federal Military Administration. The reason is that as dictated by time, they were mostly skewed towards destruction of lives. This could be speculated as the basis of nonchalance towards such technological innovations. On the other hand, it could be argued that Biafra demised with the end of hostilities in 1970. For the Military Administration not to accept Biafran technological innovations that marvelled the outside world especially when Biafra had become an integral part of Nigeria was hard to justify. It was a sort of self rejection. This self rejection has made a mockery of General Gowon's apparent honest assertion at the end of hostilities that there was "No Victor, No Vanquished." Such lack of recognition was a loss of a blessing or golden opportunity.

In order to make the basis of the secessionist technological innovations' rejections by the Federal Military Administration clearer, this study has chosen to point at specific instances of omissions in the National Development Plans of the Military Administration era as well as expressions from the military and civilian quarters. A careful study of the Military Administration era Development Plans and Progress Reports reveals inordinate emphasis given to the transfer of foreign technologies into Nigeria from abroad rather than development of indigenous technologies. In other words, despite the new sense of direction revealed by the Nigerian civil war with respect to the country's technological advance, the Military felt more comfortable to return to Nigeria's pre-civil war status quo. The inward looking policy of the secessionists was scorned. But it should be pointed out that it was the adoption of inward-looking rather than outward looking, as the Biafran Military Administration had done, which has made Japan, China and Taiwan technologically advanced. It is surprising why this lesson eluded the Military Administration.

Another angle exists by which the military import of technology rather than development of war-revealed indigenous technology can be criticized. Any technology which does not recognize the religious, cultural, geographic, and economic values and needs of a people is likely to run into serious problems and therefore unsuitable to the people. Such has been true with foreign designed technology for Nigeria's use. Such technology is usually based on the foreign author's feelings of what he thinks Nigeria needs rather than on what Nigeria feels it needs. It is the indigenes who would design technologies on what they need. This is what the Biafran achievement has presented to Nigeria. But the latter Military Administration has thrown it away. It is possible that the Military Administration was not aware of this implication of transfer of technology from outside Nigeria that it championed.

One more angle from which the Military acceptance of the transfer of technology into Nigeria could be questioned exists. It is a big question if imported technology really promotes the well-being of the recipient. This statement is contingent upon the fact that technology is a great national secret which countries doggedly conceal even from friendly nations not to talk of ideologically and militarily opposing nations. In other words, no nation has yet been found altruistic enough to export its technology to a country which will one day rival it. The validity of all these assertions is that America's present day refusal to ship its gas pipe-lines to the Soviet Union is not based on hatred but on self protection. Having analyzed the implications of the Military Administration's approach to technological advance rather than that suggested by the secessionist experience during the civil war, one may not be very wrong if one sees its approach as a poor avenue to technological self-reliance (Kirk-Greene and Rimmer, 1978)[3].

A different instance to support the assertion that the post civil war Military Administration did not accept the possibilities of technology development of Nigeria as revealed by the secessionist Biafra war era approach is found in military expression attributed to Colonel Joseph Garba. The latter was reported to have said during his lecture at the University of Nigeria, Nsukka that the neocolonialists ill-advised General Yakubu Gowon not to recognize and promote Biafran war era technological innovations for the sheer reason that such would be encouraging the rebels' innovations. One accepting this statement must do so with a grain of salt, especially since it was claimed to have come from Nsukka which was formerly in the secessionist Biafra. However, if the statement is true, it goes to show how the necolonialists tried to guard their technological superiority and transfer of obsolete technologies.

The third instance to support the assertion that the post civil war Military Administration did not welcome certain Biafran war era technologies is traceable in the Military's attitude to science and technology. One can say that the Administration's attitude to science and technology was one of subtle repression rather than recognition. Plans and Progress Reports have no indications where Nigerian scientists had been encouraged to use Biafra's indigenous technology as a pedestal for a take-off. Even the explicit or at least implicit manifestations by scientists, institutions, individuals, and groups of ex-Biafra of interest to further research in Biafra's war era technological innovations for the benefit of the country have not been encouraged. Consequently, such innovations have been allowed to languish.

The last of possible bases for the Military Administrations failure to recognize the importance of secessionist Biafra's war era technological achievements lay in the Administrations possible ignorance of the role of universities. A fact in many advanced countries is that the university is the citadel for research in technology. Many universities and institutions in the country in general, and in the war-torn former Biafra in particular, wanted to conduct research to improve war era technological achievements. These universities especially those in the war-torn area were starved of funds. Consequently, they could not do anything. The Military Administration could be excused from this accusation on the ground that it might not know the importance of the universities in technology advancement. This may be true as universities of technology were set up only after the military has relinquished power to the civilian administraiton.

In summary, it can be said that the Military Administration accepted only those secessionist Biafran war-era tested technological innovations that were not directly military-oriented and rejected those that had military overtone. Since Biafra existed only historically the Military should have accepted too all militarily biased technological innovations. By rejecting them, they have rejected according to Ottemberg (1959)[4] vital receptivity to change indispensable to rapid technological progress. The military has rejected its hard work. The military has rejected itself. The military has blocked its own technological progress.

ii. *The Federal Civilian Government Period 1979-1983*

The preceding section of this chapter has tried to analyze the post civil-war Military Government's perspectives and absorptions of the secessionist Biafran war-induced technological innovations. To make this analysis all embracing and up to date, it is reasonable to examine the efforts of the post civil-war Federal Civilian Government in its bid to technologically advance Nigeria, to see how much either implicitly or explicitly it has absorbed any of the secessionists war-induced technological innovations.

Before the real analysis of the post civil war Federal Civilian Government attitude to Biafra's war-induced technological innovations is undertaken, it is advisable to point out the unique expectation of the Federal Civilian Government. An incontrovertible fact is that in general a civilian government is more tolerant of new ideas than would be a military government. The latter is more cautious, to avoid changing the status quo; for rapid revolutionary modernization might precipitate internal strife. Therefore, the right place to look for quick technological change is not with the Federal Military Government but with the Federal Civilian Government. Given this predisposition, one would expect its greater reception of the secessionist

Biafra's war induced technological innovations than its predecessor would. It is in this vein or frame of mind that this work analyzes the post civil-war Federal Nigerian Civilian Government's policy with a view to detecting how far either explicitly or at least implicitly it has mirrored Biafran war-era approach to technological progress.

Tracing a linkage between Biafra's war-era technological innovations and the policies of the Federal Nigerian Civilian Government of the Second Republic is an irksome task that saps the energy of an analyst. Nevertheless, a search for it is called for. Whereas direct links are not easy to come by, indirect and tangential links do exist. These are traceable in the Federal Civilian Government's Outline to the Fourth National Development Plan 1981-85, and in Government Enactments and Policies since the return to civilian adminsitration in 1979.

A new development of focus which occurred with the return to power of the Federal Civilian Administration was the birth of the Federal Ministry of Science and Technology. A careful examination of the aims and objectives of this Ministry reveals that it has a lot in common with Biafra's war-induced Research and Production (RAP). Both are scientific groups charged with the function of expediting technological innovations. But RAP is a precursor of the Ministry of Science and Technology. One may not be very wrong if one concludes that the Federal Civilian Administration took the cue for the Ministry from the Biafran RAP. The Outline of the Fourth National Development Plan has credited the Federal Civilian government with allocating ₦600 million of the Plan's ₦82 billion budget to science and technology (Federal Ministry of Planning, no date)[6]. However the Federal Civilian Government has to be criticised from one angle. Whereas the Ministry solicits advice from scientists and technologists, liaises with universities and polytechnics on how to transfer technology into the country though in an undynamic and unpragmatic approach like the Federal Military government, the approach is quite atypical to the Biafran approach. It has to be added that even the allocated ₦600 million was too trivial to get the country started. Furthermore while emphasis on science and technology could be speculated to have been copied from Biafra's experience, the thrust given to the imports of foreign technologies in the Outline and the low weight of 0.7% of the planned budget given to science and technology are by no means the sure route to rapid technological advance of Nigeria. A much more ambitious amount and approach for effective and efficient stimulation of the economy are desired. No wonder why the post Civil War Federal Civilian Administration has earned criticisms for series of reductions in the universities' research grants.

It was pointed out above that the Federal Civilian Government concept of technological growth is that foreign technologies should be imported and used in the country. One can argue from this concept that the Government has not recognized the art of stimulating technological progress within, as was done by the secessionists Biafra. The Federal Civilian Government approach is a weak approach. Indices of the weakness are registered in constraints to the assimilation of such imported technologies noted here and there all over the country in the forms of lack of spare parts, lack of technical skill to maintain transferred technologies, and inacceptabilities by the people of new technologies because of cultural reasons. Implicit in the above indices is a question as to whether the continued Federal Civilian Government adherence to the policy of imported technology is not a political gimmick or manoeuvre. If it is neither then it could be inferred tha tthe Federal Civilian Government has not discovered from the secessionist Biafran examples the invaluable role stimulation of technological progress from within would play in the country's technological progress. The Biafran example is reminiscent of the Japanese approach. The latter adopted a policy of inward-looking and mind-searching, refined her indigenous technology so much that Japan ranks among the leading technologically advanced nations of the world. The sarcasms with which Japanese products were treated in the forties and the fifties are history today.

Criticisms exist against Federal Civilian Government policy of patronizing import of foreign technologies. However many critics are apprehensive to articulate them. But reasons muted for the patronage include the risk of loss of ten percent contract kickback which surreptitiously accrue to those policy makers who approve the imported foreign technologies and the feeling of pride in accepting proven indigenous technologies from ex-rebels. While the latter entertainers are guilty of not knowing that Biafra no longer exists and that technology being diffusive is indiscriminate of sectoral boundaries, the former class constitutes of rotten eggs that must be got rid of if the country will ever progress technologically.

If one were to go through the concept of technological progress of the Outline of the Fourth National Development Plan presented above, one would see the Federal Civilian Government plan as an apparent sugar-coated manifesto. Its apparent deceit lies in the absence of indices to internatize, consummate, and commercialize what has been locally achieved no matter how crude and where developed within the country. It must be pointed out that by this attitude, the Federal Civilian Government is non-chalant not only to Biafra's war era proven technological innovations but to innovations in other parts of the country. In other words, it appears the government is not encouraging indigenous innovators enough.

It appears the conclusion given above is too drastic. However the author does not think so. The reason is that specific instances exist in the Outline of the Fourth National Development Plan to buttress the conclusion. The following paragraphs will analyze specifics in the Outline to buttress the conclusion.

iii. *Specifics: Linkages of Biafran Technologies in the Fourth National Development Plan Outline*

In order to make the general conclusion given above more comprehensible this analysis goes into specifics. It takes each of the aspects of the secessionist Biafran technological innovations as classified in Chapter III and traces their linkages in the Outline of the Fourth National Development Plan, Government Enactments and Policies since the civilian rule began in October 1979.

a. *Engineering Technology.* The first area to search for technological linkages between what the rebel Biafrans did and what the Federal Civilian Administration of the post war era planned to do is in engineering technology. This field encompasses efforts made and policies adopted to promote various aspects of engineering technology such as mechanical, electrical and civil technologies. It appears that the Nigerian post-war national planners were influenced in this choice by the visible ever widening gap in engineering technology between the advanced countries and the developing countries, one of which Nigeria is. But the main question before these planners is how this technological malaise or crisis could be controlled. Should it be settled without soliciting outside help or not? A prerequisite to answering the above quesiton and finding the remedial action is the honest recognition that the malaise or crisis is of our own making. This statement derives from the already Biafran revealed cases of the country being endowed with a lot of local inputs for progress in engineering technology. But the country is not using them as the secessionist Biafra did when it was blockaded (See Chapter III). The counntry's failure has its basis in the policy of inhibiting indigenous though primordial route to promoting engineering technology. There is no doubt at all that the primordial route to engineering technology is not the best route to follow. Nevertheless, for the poor technologically-based country like Nigeria, it should be the stem on which transferred technologies in mechanical, electrical, and chemical engineering industries should be grafted. Transferred technologies as solicited for by the Outline, such as those technologies in iron and steel, building and construction equipment, communication systems, oil and petrochemical, to mention but few should be grafted on locally developed technologies. Biafra, like Japan and the Peoples Republic of China, took this approach during its difficult day and succeeded. The success marvelled the advanced world. Why the Federal Civilian Government has not recognized this route now that Biafra is an integral part of Nigeria is hard to understand.

One can speculate on the causes. speculation attributes causes to lack of pride in what we can do and stigmatization of our products as inferior to the products of other countries. To be specific, the Defence and Security sector of the country is where the actors glory in carrying well polished foreign made guns and displaying the best ironed uniforms. Such a sector as far as Nigeria is concerned is unproductive in peace time. The need to make these actors productive dictates giving them professional training. Within the Army there should be established the Army Corps of Engineers who will use the abundant local resources to fabricate gadgets and military hardwares, build army barracks, construct roads and bridges, all various aspects of engineering technology. The Outline of the Fourth National Development Plan has placed a low ceiling for the Defence and Security sector by not demanding anything more than display of well polished foreign guns and well ironed uniforms. Such a low demand has dampened the ambitions of the actors. Furthermore, the Outline has upheld the long-existing water-tight compartment between the few existing Nigerian military industries and the private civilian industries. Biafra's achievement of a certain measure of engineering progress was to a certain extent due to lack of such compartmentalization. For in Biafra, private and military industries produced engineering products that were mutually beneficial. The technology of building the secessionist Biafran gun-boats had its base in the building of pre-war fishing boats around Opobo. That technology had already stimulated the boat builders of the war era into venturing for more advanced ideas in naval architecture. The Outline of the Fourth National Development Plan failed to recognize such indigenous technological achievement even though it seems obvious that recognition and promotion of such industry will help the country's nascent fishing industry. The post civil-war Federal Civilian Government emphasis on foreign boats for trawling seems a slap in the face of the country's local boat building industry especially when such boats trawl close to the shores.

The next aspect of engineering to be analyzed is a mixed-bag of civil and electrical perspective. It was shown in Chapter III that tinkering with what ever came their way led the secessionist Biafrans to much success during the civil war. Tinkering led them to improvisation and consequently technological innovations for which the innovators received nothing but verbal ovations. Today abundant costless inputs like saw-mill wood dust, the lop-tops and branches of trees, guinea corn straws, rice husks, palm fronds, corn stalks, elephant grass, and ground nut shells which form good base materials for radio, television, and cabinet paste board industries exist. While the Outline of the Fourth National Development Plan of the Federal Civilian Administration is given a credit for recognizing their existence as useful inputs, the plan is not specific on how they can be put into use. It should have used incentives to encourage private interests into tinkering with them as tinkering was done in the ex-Biafra. Such would lead to innovations.

Another technology which the Outline of the Fourth National Development Plan seemed to have neglected was the manufacture of agricultural machinery and equipment to suit rural life and development. The Outline tended to condone the imports of tractors and other gadgets with foreign specifications rather than design and develop tools that work with or without power, given the rural setting and the unreliability of power in the country. It has to be pointed out that unless for certain parts of the country, tractors tear up the soil and create the problem of soil erosion. Biafra on the other hand paid attention to agricultural innovations.

b. *Chemical Technology.* An angle from which the Outline of the Fourth National Development Plan could be analyzed is from the promotion of chemical technology point of view. One fact of the Outline is the manifestation of interest to promote chemical technology. The emphasis of this promotion has been on promotion through imports rather than through indigenous development. The plan condones the importation of table salt, fertilizer, refined petroleum, pesticides, paint and other chemical products whereas the civil war has helped us to prove that we can produce them locally with the abundant local resources and the high level brain power available. If nothing, at least hardship induced by encirclement and blockade pressurized the Biafran scientists during the civil war to produce table salt, refined petrol, and produce explosives. Hardships made them to think constructively and work constructively. It is difficult to come to the conclusion that the authors of the Outline were not aware of these proven chemical technological bases. It is very likely they were aware. Paying no attention to them or simply glossing over them as the Outline has done seems an open slight on our capability. The slight derives from aforementioned obsession of our planners and political leaders to imported technology. To espouse exotic technologies which are at variance with our culture, environment, and values is the surest way to dwarf the country's economic progress. And this is what the Federal Civilian Government has done possibly without knowing it.

Another angle from which the Outline of the Fourth National Development Plan put out by the Federal Civilian Government could be criticized is from its poor funding of universities for research. Implicit in this statement is the fact that there was not much fund for research in chemical technology. Lack of funds discouraged self-sacrifice and hard work, the necessary prerequisites to innovative success. War spurred oneness and hardened spirit among the Biafrans. It made them take risks with explosives and dangerous chemicals. The war is no longer with us, nor do we want it any more. The Outline should have come up with a quasi means of instilling into people self-sacrifice, hard work, and risk-taking. And this should have been in the form of reasonable research grant. The Outline has rather trimmed it down and discouraged research in chemical technology.

Having seen the limitations of the Outline in promoting chemical technological innovations, it appears reasonable to say that the country needs a better shock for chemical technological innovations than can be infused by imported exotic technology. Such a shock will resurrect the war-era type of Biafran spirit of perseverence, adroitness and risk-taking which has been unwittingly ignored. It will also encourage chemical technological take-off. This type of Biafran technological spin-off is obviously very supportive of the country's national goal, namely to quickly become technologically advanced. To support the utilization of the Biafran war-era type of approach to chemical technological progress, this work agrees with Harmond (1979)[7] who emphasizes that indigenous technology rather than imported technlogy which ignores social, cultural, economic, and political climate of an area should be espoused. This the Federal Civilian Government Plan-Outline seemed to have ignored.

If we take the Biafran war era achievements as an index, it could be said that Nigeria can on its own produce plastics, electric switches, and electric sockets from the by-products of the petrol bush refinery; we can even develop our bush refinery to compete with foreign manufactured refineries being used in the country. All that can be said is that the country has achieved a base for take-off in chemical technology without knowing it.

If one were to use the Outline to draw inference, it could be inferred that the Federal Civilian Government of the post civil war has not awakened to the urgency to develop its indigenous engineering technologies based on available local resources. Such technologies are tailored to the needs and potentials of the country and will be very solid. Honest Nigerians brand this failure a delay tactic that does not like to take cognizance of the country's cultural, political and economic heritage. While Nigeria slights antiques which would have been their bases for take-off, other advanced countries praise and encourage Nigeria for the action, a deceptive tactic so that it may not develop.

c. *Welfare Promoting Technology:* This aspect of linkage is very broad. It includes those innovations which the Biafrans claimed to have made during the civil war in food, feed, clothing, medicine and shelter. One should expect a wholesale absorption of innovations in this area since they make life more enjoyable. Furthermore, they are not war oriented. It has to be pointed out that because of the preoccupations of the secessionist biafrans, they had not much to give in the form of welfare legacy. Nevertheless, the dents they made into it are worth searching for in the Outline of the Fourth National Development Plan of the Federal Civilian Government. For they are worthy of emulation.

Given the nature of food technological innovations made by the Biafrans, it will be wise to say that one finds it very difficult to make any categorical statements about their linkages existing in the Outline of the Fourth National Development Plan. Nevertheless, there are insertions in the Outline which are similar to the Biafran claims. The Outline encourages the production of early maturing food crops, multiple cropping per year, new hybrids of maize, rice and beans through cross fertilization. The civil war era's Land Army has metermorphised into the Green Revolution. Just like the secessionist Biafra, the Federal Civilian Administration in the Outline calls for increased food supply through national self-supply policy to avoid over-dependence on food imports. Food processing like dry-packing is still with us. It can be said that there is a tenuous linkage of the above Federal Civilian Government adoptions in what the Biafrans claimed to have innovated during the civil war. However, there is an area where Biafra had shed some light which the Federal Civilian Administraiton's Outline of the Fourth National Development Plan is silent. The plan has not recognized the implicit importance of water to rural farmers. Otherwise, it would have recommended supplying rural farmers with wells and canals for miniature irrigations. Its recommendations for food processing of tubers, grains and fruits are nothing to be proud about.

Another area to trace for the linkage between what the Federal Civilian Government advocated and Biafra's welfare innovations is in the means to provide protein—an indispensable human requirement. The Federal Civilian Government· like its predecessor, the secessionist Biafran Government, acclaimed domestic production of protein not only through the encouragement of backyard poultry farming but also by encouraging large scale farming. It must be said that the Government unwisely made credits available to large scale farmers and ignored entirely the small scale backyard farmers who need help most. They are also people whose shortages of protein nutrients are most acute today. Though such protein production has been encouraged, the Outline based the increased production on imported feed. In so doing the Federal Civilian government has not recognized the Biafran tested and proven production of feed from God-given, locally available, abundant and costless acacia. This technology is no where reflected in the Outline either as an area for further research or an innovation to be consummated.

The Federal Civilian Government emphasis on pharmaceutical research into the use of local inputs in drug manufacture seems to indicate its recognition of what the secessionist scientist did during the civil war. The latter used "eupatorium odoratum" to innovate vitamins. The Outline had a goal of 50% manufacture of drugs locally, but there is no effort to meet the goal. A case to support this statement is that the Federal Civil Administration's call on the country's universities in 1981-82 for survey of the country's pharmaceutical capabilities has been carried out. But nobody hears anything about the implementation of the findings. Rather it wants to meet its needs by championing the importation of drugs to the tune of 90% of its needs (Federal Ministry of Planning, no date)[8]. All that one can say is that the Outline has not recognized what potentials the Biafran claim has for the country's drug requirements. To recommend the import of 90% of the country's drug requirements for preventive, communicable, and environmental diseases is a scorn to our indigenous scientists and their claimed achievements.

d. *Shelter Technology.* One area in which the secessionist Biafrans scored some visible success was in housing technology. This is the construction of ultramodern structures out of local materials. There is no gainsaying that this innovation would improve welfare. One cannot say that the post civil war Nigeria is not suffering from housing shortages especially when high rents, costly houses, and expensive imported inputs are with us. The causal factor is that greater emphasis is placed on houses being built with imported materials than with local inputs. One would have expected the Outline of the Fourth National Development to seriously emphasize housing based on local inputs. But it does not. The inputs used by the secessionists are still with us. However, greater emphasis on imported inputs has relegated tapping the former to the background. To be specific, many of the Federal Housing Projects are nothing but match boxes and are of substandard built with imported cement and aluminum sheets. Our urban centres are adorned with cement-block quasi skyscrapers reminiscent of New York. Even the so called rural areas or villages are rapidly following suit. However, unlike the New York skyscrapers, Nigerian quasi skyscrapers in the urban and rural centres are unfortunately devoid of lifts, running water, fire and hazard escape devices. The grounds around them consist of nothing but dumping grounds for breeding flies, roaches, and rats. And mark you, such skyscrapers are indices of development aimed at implicitly in the Outline of the Fourth National Development Plan. Because there is no emphasis on building houses that suit our culture and environment out of local inputs, one is tempted to say that the Federal Civilian Government has not learnt much from the secessionist war era housing technological innovations. For the secessionists having been cut off from the outside world by encirclement and blockade improvised their houses based on locally available inputs. They used local clay to produce bricks, ceramics, ceramic floors, sanitary equipments and ceramic wall tiles. Mere mentioning such equipment in the Outline by the Federal Civilian Government is not enough. It should sponsor projects that will produce them in large quantities in the local areas. If Nigeria had adopted the Biafran example rather than simply recognizing its existence as it seems to have done the rapid inroad being made by the imports of building materials and personnel on the country's limited foreign exchange reserves would have been significantly reduced. Furthermore the country will gain in employment and skill by using local inputs to produce its building materials.

 e. *Enactment: Austerity cum Anti Smuggling.* Austerity was a powerful force that modified the lives of the secessionist Biafrans during the civil war. Its principle was that whatever cannot be afforded must be endured. Austerity induced the secessionists to innovate alternatives so as to circumvent the lacked commodities. Whether it can be said that the Federal Civilian Government has learnt this lesson from the secessionist Biafra or not, what is certain is that the Federal Civilian Government seemed to have awakened to its importance in the 1980's. Austerity severely reduced Nigeria's import bills. It bore with it the implication that the indigenes would look for means to satisfy their desires in locally produced alternatives. This approach is very likely to promote local industry and technology. In fact, it can be called the most sane meansure taken to promote indigenous technology. One must cut one's coat according to one's size. This is what the Federal Civilian Government has done. It must be now or never. Austerity is belt-tightening now for better future.

 Following close on the heels of the austerity meansures was the Federal Civilian Government Enactment of the Anti-Smuggling Act. At its face value, the Act has promised to prohibit those imports of foreign technologies and commodities that thwart the growth of local alternatives. It seems that only an insane person would not see the auspicious technological future this Act has for the country. Having enjoyed manufactured products and having got such products taken away by the Anti-Smuggling Act, there would occur stimuli for production of local substitutes. An example to be taken from the secessionist Biafra was liquor distillation out of "mmanya ngwo" because imported liquor was no longer available. Biafra trod this path and succeeded. May or may not be that the Federal Civilian Government got its cue from the Biafran experience. This is the only hope for the country's decaying or dormant technologies. If practically implemented fully, technological progress would be inevitable. There will be reduced import bills, increased employment, improved know-how, better utilization of locally abundant inputs, and improved world image.

 One observation worth mentioning is the continued influx of manufactured imports into the country. It attests to the loopholes in the Act. There is no gainsaying that the Act was discussed and approved in the Federal House by politicians before it was handed over to the President. It is possible that whereas the President and his honest politicians discussed with honest intentions, certain of the politicians who had interests to gain from continued importation of foreign manufacturers and technologies were busy surreptitiously undermining the work of the honest politicians. Only an insane judge would expect such politicians to collaborate with the honest ones in passing an Act that would jeopardize their interests. Because this is the case, the Act should be seen only as a smoke-screen to hide the selfish ambitions and interests of callous Nigerian politicians. Anti-Smuggling Act cannot and does not encourage the growth of indigenous technology in an environment fermented with wanton chase for self-enrichment and irrationalities of callous politicians. The last statement cannot be more true elsewhere than in Nigeria.

It is not difficult to detect the hoax of the Anti-Smuggling Act of the Federal Civilian Government of the post civil war Nigeria. The common man being aware of the hoax has not taken the Act serious. Smuggling is today just as it was before the passage of the Act. Crafty customs officials and policemen, alias the common man's Federally-known licensed thieves, like the Act because it offers them an opportunity to get illicit payments from smugglers. It can be said that every banned manufactured commodity is found in abundance in the country today. One should not wonder why the common man condones smuggling if one watches the shoes and clothes that the authors of the Act put on, the gadgets they acquire in their homes, and the dishes and furniture they have acquired since the passage of the Act to understand the hoax. One has to watch the authors of the Act as they return from overseas trips to realize that with their faces turned to Nigeria, they are preaching against smuggling while the luggage which they are dragging into Nigeria are filled with foreign manufactures that hinder or discourage indigenous technological progress. Being that the common man is aware of all these, call this common man if you like, he smuggles with impunity and without conscience. If the Federal Civilian Government were serious, these unscrupulous importers must be checked first. Seriousness implies following the hardheaded burning passion of Mahatma Ghandi's type for technological self-improvement. This would create self-imposed rather than the hoax Anti-Smuggling Act. The Anti-Smuggling Act is analytically a hidden skeleton in the cupboard. It has unleashed austerity for the poor man, created a country wide inflation because of increased prices imposed by importers to cover illicit payments to the police and customs officials. While it reduces certain classes of outputs, it has not generated the much expected technological earthquake or antidote to Nigeria's malaise, namely lack of indigenous technological progress in the country.

In conclusion, one looking at the analysis of the linkages of the Biafran technological innovations in the post civil war Federal Nigerian governments Plans and Policies would no doubt describe such linkages as sporadic and tenuous. More is still required to be extracted from the proven war examples. This will allow or stimulate the use of local resources to build up an everlasting technological base. In summary this is the country's hope.

References

1. Emeka Aniagolu, "Presidential pardon: Is there a Partisan Connection?" *Nigerian Forum* (Lagos, Nigerian Institute of International Affairs, june, 1982) p. 47.
2. A.O.E. Animalu, "Model for Technology Transfer Between Nigeria and the United States of America," *Technological Development in Nigeria,* Moyibi Amoda and Cyril D. Tyson eds. (New York: Third Press International, 1979), p. 243.
3. Anthony Kirk-Green and Douglas Rimmer, *Nigeria Since 1970 A Political and Economic Outline* (London: Holder and Stoughton, 1978), p. 148.
4. Simon Ottemberg, "Ibo Receptivity to Change," *Continuity and Change in African Cultures,* Bascom W. Russell and Melville I. Herskovits eds. (Chicago, U.S.A.: The University of Chicago Press, 1959), p. 130.
5. Gleen E. Schweitzer, "Technological Transfers: The Nigerian Model," *Technological Development in Nigeria,* Moyibi Amoda and Cyril D. Tyson eds. (New York: Third Press International, 1979), p. 249.
6. Federal Ministry o f Planning, *Outline of the Fourth National Development Plan 1981-85* (Lagos, Nigeria: No date), pp. 54-55.
7. Rose W. Hammond, "Relevant Technology and the University," *Technological Development in Nigeria,* Moyibi Amoda and Cyril D. Tyson eds. (New York: Third Press International, 1979), p. 270.
8. Federal Ministry of Planning, *Guideline: Fourth National Development Plan* (Lagos, Nigeria: No date), pp. 78-79.

CHAPTER V

BASES OF FEDERAL GOVERNMENT ATTITUDE TO INDIGENOUS TECHNOLOGY: A SPECULATIVE TRIP

A fact that Chapter III has tried to prove is that crude indigenous technologies existed in pre-civil war Nigeria. This assertion on investigation seems to be supportive by historical records. For the Nigerian history books abound with documentations such as those on the morocan leathers of Katsina in Northern Nigeria, the "ashoke" textile products of Oyo in Western Nigeria, the Ife bronze products of Western Nigeria, the ebony carved products of Benin in Mid-Western Nigeria, the glass beads of Bida in Northern Nigeria, and the ironworks of Awka in Eastern Nigeria, all products of crude indigenous technologies. The chapter envisaged the civil war as calamitous, whose only advantage though tangential lay in creating a greater awareness for the indigenous technologies of the former Eastern Nigeria, alias the secessionist Biafra of the Nigerian civil war. In other words, the Biafran secessionist war was at best only an instrument of focusing greater attention and awareness on the indigenous technologies of only the former Eastern Nigeria. The implication is that if the civil war had been fought either in the Northern or Western Nigeria, it is likely that such awareness as was created in the case of Biafra would have been created too.

In contrast to Chapter III, the next chapter which is Chapter IV accepted the secessionist Biafran technologies as having been exposed and improved upon by war pressure. But it then went on to trace the receptivity of such indigenous technologies in the post civil war government plans and policies. The findings had not been very encouraging; at best they could be described as only sporadically encouraging. In other words, the linkages between the war era secessionist technological innovations and the post civil war plans and policy adoptions of the Federal Governments had been very tenuous. Such a treatment of indigenous technologies had not only caused great consternation to the honest Nigerians but also had been echoed by prejudiced Nigerians as a criticism for non-acceptance of the ex-rebel's technological achievements.

This chapter accepts the last statement of the last chapter as a negligible causal factor to the flimsy acceptance. Therefore, by taking a diametrically opposed stand, it focuses attention on the chief causal factors rather than that recognized by prejudiced critics. The search reveals economic, psychological, sociological administrative or institutional, and technological constraints subtly programmed into the economy by years of colonial rule. The people have reacted in conformity with the programming without recognizing the deterrent forces. To prove this charge, this work takes each of the programmed point up for a critical analysis. It will seek for the inhibiting factors, suggests means of subdueing them in order to arouse interest in upholding indigenous technologies. The solution to Nigeria's technological problems can only be discovered if their programmed bases are first carefully analyzed.

It has to be pointed out that there is nothing intuitively wrong with being a colony except that the indigenes of the colony are groomed to accept, hook and sinker, alien technological structures inclucated into them through a form of international relations. People are programmed in such a way that they seek manufactures of industrial products. The theory made Nigeria to specialize where specialization counted less whereas Great Britain, Nigeria's metropolis specialized where spcialization counted more. The technological constraint of this economic programming derived from the fact that Great Britain had treated Nigeria as an alien to whom the technology of refining and manufacturing the raw materials must never be made available. Even efforts at promoting indigenous technology in the process of those raw materials must be discouraged at all costs. Because the manufactured products were dumped in Nigeria, the incentive and pressure to improve on the indigenous technology received less steam. It was through this looking glass that Nigeria saw technological advance until the outbreak of the civil war. It is a sheer mistake to think that the war experience would change this perspective of technology in the post civil war Nigeria. The reason is that habits once formed are difficult to relinquish. This programmed economic constraint of the colonial era is responsible for non-acceptance of those technological innovations by the post civil war Federal Nigerian Government which war pressure induced the secessionist Biafra to make. The only way out is for Nigeria to realize that the theory of comparative advantage as it exists now is not to its technological interest. Doggedly following it will constrain it to be perpetually backward technologically. It is imperative that the country takes a skeptical look at the theory of comparative advantage, look inward, resurrect and update its ambitions and values which they do not know are unsuitable to their interest. Such ambitions and values inevitably suit the aspirations of the metropolis. The indigenes see any deviation from the programming as bad, unacceptable and must be annihilated. it is in this predicament that the post civil war Nigerian Governments have found themselves. Programmed colonial factors have been significantly instrumental to the sporadic acceptance of the secessionist technological innovations. It is not as the prejudiced but vocal critics of non-acceptance have asserted. Bauer (1979)[1] however does not see any inbuilt constraints in colonial programming. In his own concept colonialism is rather stimuli infusing. He argues that a comparative analysis of the colonies with non-colonial developing countries would show the former progressing faster and therefore proves his case. In order to understand how colonial programming had created constraints to indigenous technological innovation, it pays to make a critical analysis of each aspect of programmed constrain into the pre-independence colonial Nigeria.

i. *Economic Constraint:* Nigeria as a satellite of Great Britain adopted capitalism. One legacy of capitalism which was inimical to the technological advancement of Nigeria is the theory of comparative advantage. This theory confined Nigeria in her pre-war era to the producer of raw materials with not more than the primitive technology. These raw materials were destined to the technologically advanced Britain to be used in dormant indigenous technologies. This is its easiest avenue to a lasting technological progress.

ii. *Psychological Constraints:* Psychological constraint to acceptance of war induced secessionist technological innovations originated in the pre-civil war colonial control of the minds of the Nigerians. The people were programmed to think and feel in a manner in consonance with the metropolis' ambitions and aspirations. There is no gainsaying that the predominant feeling in pre-civil war Nigeria was that British values were incomparably superior to those of Nigeria. This feeling was subtly sunken into the people through the mode of colonial education prevailing in Nigeria. It can therefore be inferred from this perspective that the people were entrapped unknowingly into accepting the programmed values and technologies of Britain to the detriment of their indigenous technologies. Such brain manipulation implied the rejection of opponents to programmed constraints even if such opponents were good. Any society or sector of the society that rejects the programmed constraint is deviant to be quashed. This has been the predicament in which the secessionist Biafra, alias former Eastern Nigeria, found itself. This may provide the justification for British participation in suppressing the secessionist Biafra. It may provide the rationale for the limited influence of much of the secessionist technological innovations in the post civil war plans and policies of Federal Nigeria. The root cause of rejection, therefore, is not rebellious rank of the secessionist Biafra to Nigeria but that such a rebellion in the long run will jeopardize the technological ambitions of Britain in Nigeria.

iii. *Technological Constraint:* One constraint that was very instrumental to rejecting the secessionist war induced technological innovations in Nigeria is due to technological manipulation of pre-civil war Nigeria. The study of practical or industrial arts of the type that would promote the country's technological progress was shilly shally in the pre-independence Nigeria. The country was furnished with technological products and equipment without being taught how either to duplicate them or even use them efficiently. Even spare parts for the repair of such technological products were lacking. Indigenous efforts to promote technologies were subtly discouragd by the incomparability of the indigenous products with those of foreign technologies. That the secessionist technological innovations were rejected implicitly in the post civil war plans and policies derives from the colonial legacy of the sense crudity. The progress technologically a people must be proud of its products, no matter how crude. And this is what is lacking in the post civil war Nigerian Governments.

iv. *Sociological constraint:* The fourth constraint emanating from the colonial programming of Nigeria that led to nonchalance attitude to civil war induced technological innovations in the country is sociological. The pre-independence administration could not be said to have understood the science of human society, the organizations and relations of such a society as Nigeria. One could speculate that the reason is that Britain, the imperial government, came from a distant land with different ideals and values. Whatever might be the reason, the sociological programming of Nigeria sowed the seeds of conditions unfavourable to technological progress. In fact, such unfavourable conditions created relations that led to the civil war. The programming subtly harped on tribal dominations and hatred; it can be inferred that these two obnoxious stimuli actually destabilized rather than stabilized Nigeria. Bauer (1979)[2] has controverted the implications of the sociological programming. He called it euphemistically a major legacy of the colonial legacies. It is agreed that it is a major legacy. But is a major negative legacy from the technological ambitions of Nigeria.

The colonial societal programming can be criticized from another angle. It was a programme that deprived the Nigerians a sense of direction. People were organized and educated in such a way that they did not realize that imported technologies were inimical to local technologies and that it was against their long-run technological interest to depend on imports rather than manufacture. For if they realized the inherent dangers of import dependency, they would automatically adopt an attitude negative to import dependency. In a way, it can be inferred that the pre-independence societal programming has left most Nigerians, especially the politicians, incapable of understanding anything about technology. They have not been induced to see positive relationship between internal technological development and reduced dependence on imported manufactures. Otherwise, they would have welcomed the secessionist Biafran revelation with relief. If we follow Baran (1957)[3], we might conclude that the societal programming in Nigeria by colonial Britain was the cause of the misery and stagnation that befell Nigeria during the civil war. Nigeria would have progressed faster than it is now if the civil war had not occurred. From this constraint point of view, colonial sociological programming which was expected to be a mighty engine of technological progress in Nigeria has become a great hurdle to technological advance, causing abysmal squalor, conflicts, misery and hopelessness in the society. The secessionist Biafran war-induced indigenous technological innovations were not sporadically adopted in the post civil war plans and policies of Nigeria not because of any dislike of the source of the innovations but because the society had been groomed in a way not to trust one another's innovations during the colonial era.

v. *Administrative or Institutional Constraint:* One more colonial originated constraint contributory to sporadic acceptance of the secessionist Biafran technologies in Federal Nigerian Government post civil war plans and policies derived from the residual administrative or institutional legacies. Political independence as we today see it seems unreal especially when the alien administrative or institutional forces that came with colonialism have not yet been dismantled. The alien forces have destroyed Nigeria's ideology of crude production without giving it a new ideology which would emphasize methods to improve crude indigenous technologies. As capital never falls from heaven, any meaningful administrative or institutional machinery should foster the means where-by capital for technological progress should be made possible. It is through abstention or self-sacrifice; and the pre-independence machinery never did emphasize such. Biafra's experience was a challenge to this institutional set-up for it emphasized self-sacrifice for technological progress. It was a new ideology that exhumed dormant indigenous technologies, opened the door for unavailable foreign technologies, taught how to replicate the foreign technologies with local inputs, and harnessed human talents and energy so as to increase the national cake. Unfortunately the pre-independence colonial administrative set-up had no room for this.

Another angle from which the administrative programming set-up could be criticized is from the policy point of view. The Federal Government policy of banning imports has somewhat a retarding effect on technological innovations in Nigeria. Banning is visible and may be retaliatory. Though it may reduce foreign exchange losses it is only a short run antidote to monetary problems. But it leads to decline in foreign technologies to be available for replication. A better alternative is the creation of socio-political framework that automatically de-emphasizes the importance of foreign goods and at the same time directs attention to local products. If this administration or institutional orientation had existed at the end of the war, the secessionist technological innovations would have found acceptance. This should therefore be the thrust of Nigerian orientation for stable technological advance. It is likely to promote the country's technological progress.

References

1. P. T. Bauer *Desent on Development* (Cambridge, Mass.: Harvard University Press, 1979), pp. 149-151.
2. Ibid. p. 155.
3. Paul A. Baran *Political Economy of Growth* (New York: Monthly Review Press, 1957), pp. 249-250.

SUMMARY AND CONCLUSION

Wars are a shock to nations. They force them to rise up and do something to defend themselves. The doing of something to defend oneself is the first step to technological advance. Though war stimulates technological progress, it is an evil that must never be condoned. Nigeria unfortunately experienced one in the second half of the 1960's with tangential positive technological advantages. Such advantages were in various aspects of engineering, agricultural, and welfare promoting technological developments.

One would have expected a wholesale post-war Nigerian Government absorption and assimilation of such innovations. But that had not been the case. The failure had led to speculations on a multitude of causal factors ranging from ethnicity to domination, hatred, and fears. Undoubtedly these are causal factors; but they are slim causal factors which in themselves had not enough steam for the type of assimilation.

A careful and deeper study of history has revealed the causes of the flimsy and sporadic acceptance of the secessionist war-induced indigenous technological innovations in the pre-independence colonial programming of Nigeria by Great Britain. It was a programme that had no ideology or sense of direction. It was a programme that never prepared the people for technological advance. Given such a situation, receptivity was somewhat an anathema. Despite all that had been said, Nigeira's technological future lies in abstracting itself from the colonial programming, realistically looking at the pattern of ideology of technological progress revealed by the civil war, and using that pattern for its quick technological progress. This is its sure road to technological advance.

In conclusion this study concludes from the secessionist Biafra's revelation that there is a wealth of indigenous technological innovation possibilities existing in Nigeria today. There is a need for concerted action from the Governments, scientists, and business towards greater innovations. It will involve sacrifice from everyone in the economy. Only under the above condition could the country succeed technologically.

BIBLIOGRAPHY

1. Aniagolu, E., "Presidential Pardon: Is there a Partisan Connotation" *The Nigerian Forum* (Lagos, Nigeria: Nigerian Institute of International Affairs, June 1983).
2. Animalu, A.E.O., "Model for Technology Transfer Between Nigeira and the United States of America," *Technological Development of Nigeria* Moyibi, A. and C.D. Tyson eds. (New York: Third Press International, 1979).
3. Americana International, *Encyclopedia Americana Vol. XXVIII* Danbury, Connecticut: Americana International Corporations, 1978).
4. Branson, L. and G. Goethal eds., *Studies from Psychology, Sociology, and Anthropology* (New York: Basic Book, 1964).
5. Buchan, A., *War in Modern Society: An Introduction* (London: C. A. Watts and Company Limited, 1966).
6. Cervenka, Z., *The Nigerian War 1969-1970* (Frankfurt am Main: Bernard and Graefe Verlag Fur Wehrwesen, 1971).
7. Deane, P., "War and Industrialization," *War and Economic Development* J. M. Winters ed. (New York: Cambridge University Press, 1975).
8. Ehrman, J., *the Navy in the War of William III 1689-1698* Cambridge: Cambridge University Press, 1953).
9. Ellison, J., *Daily Express* (London: December 10, 1969).
10. Federal Ministry of Planning, *The Third National Development Plan* (Lagos, Nigeria: No Date).
11. Federal Ministry of Planning, *Guideline: Fourth National Development Plan* (Lagos, Nigeria: No Date).
12. Federal Ministry of Planning, *Outline of the Fourth National Development Plan 1981-1985* (Lagos, Nigeria: No Date).
13. Forsyth, F., *The Biafran Story* (Harmondsworth: Penguin Books, 1977).
14. Gold, H., Biafra Goodbye (San Francisco, U.S.A.: Townwindow Press, 1970).
15. Griggs, W., *Shakespeare's Merchant of Venice, The First (The Worst) Quarto* (London: William griggs, Hanover Street, Peckham S.E., 1600).
16. Hamond, R. W., "Relevant Technology and the University," *Technological Development in Nigeria* Moyibi A. and C. D. Tyson eds. (New York: Third Press International, 1979).
17. Howard, M. and P. Paret eds., *Carl von Clausewitz On War* (New Jersey: Princeton University Press, 1976).
18. John, A. H., *War and the English Economy 1700-1763* Economic History Review Series VII (1954-1955).
19. Kirk-Green, A. and D. Rimmer, *Nigeria Since 1970: A Political and Economic Outline* (London: Holder and Stoughton, 1978).
20. Lane, F. C., "Economic Consequences of Organized Violence," *Journal of*

Economic History XVIII (1958).
21. Madiebo, A., *The Nigerian Revolution and the Biafran War* (Enugu, Nigeria: Fourth Dimension Publishing Company Limited, 1980).
22. *Markpress Release* (Aba, Biafra: February 6, 1968).
23. *Markpress Release* (Aba, Biafra: February 29, 1968).
24. Mays, H. and B. M. Metzger, *The Oxford Annotated Bible (RSV) Luke IX Verse LXII* (New York: Oxford University Press, 1971).
25. Ndubisi, A. F., "Unpublished Letter to Alhaji Shehu Shagari, The President of the Federal Republic of Nigeria" (Nsukka, Nigeria: Institute of Education, University if Nigeria, Nsukka, Nigeria; March 21, 1980).
26. Nwankwo, A. A., *Nigeria: The Challenge of Biafra* (Enugu, Nigeria: Fourth Dimension Publishing Company Limited, 1972).
27. Ojukwu, O. C. *Biafra: Selected Speeches with Journal of Events* (New York: Harper and Row Publishers, 1969).
28. Okigbo, P. N., "Problem of Food Scarcity and Need for Increased Food Production in Wartime Biafra," *Seminar in Emergency Food Production* Unpublished (Afor-Ugini, Biafra: 1969).
29. Otteraberg, S., "Ibo Receptivity to Change," *Continuity and Change in African Culture* Bascom W. Russell and M. D. Herskovits eds. (Chicago, U.S.A.: The University of Chicago Press, 1959).
30. Oyinbo, J., *Nigeria: Crisis and Beyond* (London: Charles Knight and Company Limited, 1971).
31. Schweitzer, G. E., "Technological Transfer: The Nigerian Model," *Technologic Development in Nigeria* Moyibi A. and C. D. Tyson eds. (New York: Third Press International, 1979).
32. Sombart, W., *Studien Zur Entwicklungsgeschichte des Modernen Kapitalismus II Krieg und Kapitalismus* (Munich, 1913).
33. *The Biafran Sun* (Aba, Biafra: 1968-1969).
34. *The Biafran Sun* (Aba, Biafra: January 16, 1968).
35. *the Biafran Sun* (Aba, Biafra: February 28, 1968).
36. *The Biafran Sun* (Aba, Biafra: August 8, 1968).
37. *The Biafran Sun* (Aba, Biafra: November 13, 1968).
38. *The Biafran Sun* (Aba, Biafra: November 28, 1968).
39. *The Biafran Sun* (Aba, Biafra: July 3, 1969).
40. *The Washington Post* (Washington, D. C.: September 5, 1983).
41. Williams, R., *The First and Last Things* (New York: The New Thinkers Library 1964).

INDEX

Abacha, 61
Abagana, 24
Acacia, 65-66,68
Achi, 61-62
Acoia barteri, 46
Adekunle, 58
African countries, 7
Akpateshi, 49
Alcohol, 49-53
Alkalai, 54
Algae, 61
American, 13,41
   technology, 13
   spy, 13
Animal feed, 63-66
Aniagolu, 72
Animalu, 73
Anyakoha, 61
Anaba, 67
Armoured vehicles, 36-37
Army Corp of Engineers, 80
Arochukwu, 62
Asaba, 36
Asanamfor, 37
Ashoke, 88
Atlantic, 13
Attrition, 57
Austerity, 85-87
Awka, 21,88,59
Azikiwe, 17

Baran, 92
Bauer, 90,91
Battery reactivator, 38-39
Bende Agricultural Research Centre, 60
Biafra, 7-9,10-14,16-18,20,79
Biafra babies, 20
Biafra bear, 28

Biafra Bush Refinery, 39-41,45
Biafra civilian, 10,26
Biafra Chemical Scientists, 41-42
Biafra crude war-technologies, 18
Biafra entrepreneurs, 11
Biafra home-made rockets, 26
Biafra home-made weapon, 20-26
Biafra indigenous technologies, 10,88
Biafra Military Government, 59
Biafra Navy, 38
Biafra Red Devil, 37
Biafra Scientists, 12,13,43,47,48,56,67
Biafra secession, 9
Biafra Shore Battery, 34,36
Biafra Soldiers, 10,32,68
Biafra Strategies, 9-14
Biafra Starving Children, 59
Biafra Sun, 17,54,60,62-63
Bida, 88
Blockade, 11,12,57,58,60,63
Bomb, 20
Brakefluid, 48
Britain, 7,10
British Gun Cotton 43-44
Bullets, 22,67
Bush Refinery, 45-46,47

Calabar, 38,62
Cameroon, 63
Carbohydrates, 62,65,66
Caritas, 10,49,58
Cartridge, 22
Cassava, 59,64
Cast iron, 19
Castro, 68
Centre of Excellence, 73
Cervenka, 8,17,27,28,58,21,26,63

Chadian-Nigerian, 32
Chemical 22,29
  technological innovation, 41,81
Chiaka, 51,52
China, 74
Chop-one-chop-two, 63
Cigarettes, 59
Civil war, 13,14,49
  strategies, 8,9,49,81
Coffin, 28,30,33
Communist Russia, 10
Controel, 52
Conventional strategies, 9
Corn, 65,66
Cotton, 23,43
Crude indigenous scientists, 12

Daily Express, 34
Defacto, 11,12,39
Dehydrated, 65
Delayed action fuse, 19
Der Stern, 58
Diesel, 40,46
Distillation, 49
Drugs, 67,68
Dry pack, 63

Eastern Nigeria, 49,54,55,60,88
Ehrman, 14
Ellison, 34
Engine Oil, 47-48
Enugu, 21,24,28,46,72
Esilesi, 49
Eupatorium odoratum, 56,64,68,83,66
Euphemistic brawl, 10
European, 22
Ex-Biafran scientist, 49
Explosives, 27,42-43,29

Fairy Smith, 17
Federal Army, 9,10,12,37,43,46,57,58,59
  60,63,68,71,72,13,18
Federal Civilian Government, 76-79,80
  81,82,83,84
Federal Military Government, 72-76,92
Federal Navy, 59
Federal Strategies, 11
  war strategies, 9,66
Flying Ogbunigwe, 28,34
Food Production Directorate, 59,61
Food Processing, 61-63
Footcutter, 28,30,31
Foreign exchange, 12,13,69,66,85,44
Foreign technologies, 85

Garba, 75
Genocide, 37
Gold, 59
Gowon, 75
Green Revolution, 83
Griggs, 11
Gunboats, 37-38,80
Gun Powder, 19,29-30
Guns, 20-21

Hand grenade, 18-20
Harmond, 82
Helicopter, 21
Helmet, 24-26
Hitler, 17
Holocaust, 9,10
Hydroxide, 42

Ian Smith, 7
Ibo, 8,58
Icheku, 46
Ife bronze, 88
Illegal, 13
Imoke, 59
Imported technology, 91
Indigenous technology, 12,71,86,89
Induced technological innovations, 91 92

Industrial Era Dev. Co., 69
Israelites, 36

Jaggi, 63
Japan, 74,79
Japanese, 78
Jiakpu, 61
John, 14
John Holt, 56

Kai-kai, 49
Kampala, 68
Kapok, 43,44
Katsina, 88
Kennedy, 54
Kerosene, 40,46
Kirk-Greene, 75
Kontrol, 52
Kwashiokor, 59,60,63,67,61

Land Army, 59,60,73,83
Lead balls, 23,33
Lever Brothers, 48
Linkages, 71
Local raw materials, 20
Local resources, 12,13,42
Local technologies, 12,91

Madiebo, 8,13,17,20,24,27,38,46,26
Mark Press, 17,24
Middlekoop, 63
Mid-Westerners, 8
Mines, 28
Minicon, 20
Mmanya ngwo, 44,50
  nkwo, 50
Mmeme, 51-52
Mortars, 22,24
Moses, 36

Ncha, 62

New Era, 60
New York, 84
Nigerian Civil War, 7,16-17,39
Nigeria's Army, 9,22
Nigeria's First Battalion, 24
Nigeria's Army Strategies, 13
Nitric acid, 43
Nnewi, 62-63
Noko Magic Washing Powder, 53-55
Northern Nigeria, 88
Northerners, 8
Nsisa, 62
Nsukka, 37,75
Nwankwo, 8,13,46,48

Obi, 50,67
Ogbunigwe, 34,43,44
Ogogoro, 49
Ojukwu, 22,36,56
  bucket, 28,32,34,35
Ojukwu, 8,22
  kettle, 32
  teacup, 32
Okazi, 68
Okposi, 56
Old Testament, 36
Onitsha, 36,63
Onne, 37
Opobo, 80
Ore, 37
Ose oji, 52
Ossai, 64,65,66
Ottenberg, 76
Oyinbo, 8,58,68
Oyo, 88

Paraguay, 20
Permagnate potash, 64
Petrol, 19,40
  super, 46

Petroleum, 45
Port Harcourt, 37-38
Pope, 58
Potash 54
Propaganda, 9
Propellant powder, 44
Protein, 60,61,63
Push-me-I-push-you, 49

Quasi-scientists, 44

Rabbit, 60,64
Rebel, 60,63
Red Cross, 10,49,58,63
Red Sea, 36
Research and Production, 39,77,50
Research institute, 60
Rhodesia, 7
Rimmer, 75
River Niger, 49
Rockets, 26,27-28
Romans, 41
Russian Mig, 69
  Submarine, 12

Saboteurs, 12
Salad, 63
Salt, 55-57
Secessionist, 44,52
Secessionist scientists, 64
Second Republic, 77
Self-reliance, 73,75
Shrapnels, 27,29,31,33,35
Siam, 56,68,61,66
Smuggling Act, 85,86
Snails, 60,63,66
Soap, 53-55
Solanium, 61
Sombart, 13
South Korea, 13
Soviet Kalashnikov, 21

Soviet Union, 22,75,13
Steel helmet, 26
Swiss International Communities, 63

Taiwan, 74
Technological Advance, 92
Technological innovation, 71-72,76
Technological progress, 91,92
Telfiaria, 67
Toxic, 65

Ubalu, 56
Uda, 51
Udi Coalfields, 46
Uganda, 68
Ugba, 61
Ugochukwu, 39
Ukpaka, 61
Uli, 69
Umudike Research Station 60
Uniforms, 68
United Nations Delegations, 58
United States of America, 65
University of Nigeria, Nsukka, 43,75
Universities, 42
Utazi, 68
Uwaegbute, 43
Uziza, 51-52
Uzummuo, 17-18,20-22,24,27,30,36-38

Vaccine, 67
Vegetables, 67,59
Viet Cong, 41
Vietnamese War, 41

War leaders; 9
War torn, 51,76
Washington Post, 13
Western, 8,88
Women Council of Social Services, 63
World Council of Churches, 10,49,58

Yoruba, 8
Yam, 59

Zinc, 39

www.ingramcontent.com/pod-product-compliance
Lightning Source LLC
Chambersburg PA
CBHW021411290426
44108CB00010B/483